KT-520-141

THE LEARNING CENTRE
HAMMERSMITH AND WEST
LONDON COLLEGE
GLIDDON ROAD
LONDON W14 9BL

WITHDRAWN

HOUSING AND SUPPORT SERVICES FOR ASYLUM SEEKERS AND REFUGEES: A GOOD PRACTICE GUIDE

HAMMERSMITH WEST LONDON COLLEGE

342319

Available in alternative formats

This publication can be provided in alternative formats, such as large print, Braille, audiotape and on disk.

Please contact:
Communications Department,
Joseph Rowntree Foundation,
The Homestead,
40 Water End,
York YO30 6WP.
Tel: 01904 615905.
Email: info@jrf.org.uk

HOUSING AND SUPPORT SERVICES FOR ASYLUM SEEKERS AND REFUGEES: A GOOD PRACTICE GUIDE

JOHN PERRY

PUBLISHED FOR THE JOSEPH ROWNTREE FOUNDATION BY THE CHARTERED INSTITUTE OF HOUSING

The Chartered Institute of Housing
The Chartered Institute of Housing is the professional organisation for people who work in housing. Its purpose is to maximise the contribution housing professionals make to the wellbeing of communities. The Chartered Institute has over 19,000 members across the UK and the Asian Pacific working in a range of organisations, including housing associations, local authorities, the private sector and educational institutions.

Chartered Institute of Housing, Octavia House, Westwood Way, Coventry CV4 8JP
Tel: 024 7685 1700 Fax: 024 7669 5110 Website: www.cih.org

The Joseph Rowntree Foundation
The Joseph Rowntree Foundation has supported this project as part of its programme of research and innovative development projects, which it hopes will be of value to policy makers, practitioners and service users. The facts presented and views expressed in this report, however, are those of the authors and not necessarily those of the Foundation.

Joseph Rowntree Foundation, The Homestead, 40 Water End, York YO30 6WP
Tel: 01904 629241 Website: www.jrf.org.uk

Published in association with **hact (the housing associations' charitable trust)**
Hact develops solutions to issues concerning people on the margins of mainstream housing provision. For further information about hact and its refugee housing integration programme please visit www.hact.org.uk

hact, Octavia House, 50 Banner Street, London EC1Y 8TX
Tel: 020 7247 7800 Email: hact@hact.org.uk

Housing and Support Services for Asylum Seekers and Refugees: A Good Practice Guide
John Perry
© Chartered Institute of Housing 2005
1 903208 98 X

Layout by Jeremy Spencer
Cover illustration by Sandra Howgate
Printed by Genesis Print & Marketing

HAMMERSMITH
LONDON
LEARNING CENTRE

1 9 JAN 2006

342319 £22.15 £25.80

363.531 PER

Housing

Whilst all reasonable care and attention has been taken in compiling this publication, the publishers regret that they cannot assume responsibility for any error or omission that it contains. Readers should take legal, financial and other appropriate advice before taking any specific action in relation to this subject.

All rights reserved. No part of this publication may be reproduced, stored in a retrieval system or transmitted in any form or by any means, electronic, mechanical, photocopying, recording, or otherwise without the prior permission of the publishers.

342319

CONTENTS

FOREWORD

The issue of how we house and provide support services to new migrants – whether asylum seekers, refugees, or people who come here to work – should be high up the agenda of housing organisations. The make up of those who are homeless, or living in poor conditions, or needing some kind of ongoing support, is changing in many cities and even smaller towns.

In part, this is because government policy is placing asylum seekers in places as different as Bury, Glasgow, Derby and Peterborough – often shifting their ethnic composition and service needs. In part it is because people are choosing to settle – or look for work – in many different parts of the UK. As recent research has shown, in doing so they are likely now or in the future to contribute to the economic vitality of the places to which they go.

Obviously, having somewhere decent to live is likely to be their first priority. But they will also need health care, perhaps training, a job, a school for their children. Housing organisations are well-placed to identify the need for and perhaps set up or create partnerships to provide these wider support services. And it is vital that they do so if people who are new to communities are to integrate into them.

It is essential for housing organisations working in areas with significant asylum seeker and refugee populations, to understand fully the needs of different households, working with and through refugee community organisations wherever possible.

At the Housing Corporation we are keen to get this message across to housing associations, and have recently published our own report *Still Surviving, Now Settling*, which shows how they can respond. It is one of the issues dealt with in our BME action plan for 2005-08, and one we hope will feature in BME strategies at local level.

We therefore welcome this new guide from the Joseph Rowntree Foundation and Chartered Institute of Housing, as it goes into the practical detail which complements our wider study. It is also UK wide – reflecting government policy and practice.

I have no hesitation in commending the guide and hope not only that it will be widely read but that it will help in the drive to get housing organisations much more actively engaged in providing services which – as the guide shows – are already in place in some areas, but not yet widely enough.

Jon Rouse
Chief Executive, Housing Corporation

ACKNOWLEDGEMENTS

The idea for this guide came from discussions with five people closely concerned with the issues – Heather Petch at hact, Ann Branson at Leicester City Council, Sandra Skeete at Refugee Housing Association, Celia Cashman at Safe Haven Yorkshire and Alison Jarvis at the Joseph Rowntree Foundation – who also gave invaluable help as the work proceeded.

The advisory group, several of whom made detailed comments, were:

Michael Collins	consultant (formerly of the Scottish Refugee Council)
Santino Deng	New Hope Refugee Partnership
Jennifer Harris	University of York
Kurshida Mirza	Housing Corporation
Deborah Quilgars	University of York
Ian Simpson	Bradford Community Housing Trust
Rachel Westerby	Refugee HA
Ephreme Woube	Ethiopian Community in Britain

Sam Lister at CIH collaborated on the guide and produced the detailed material on homelessness and lettings. Bob Blackaby gave helpful comments on chapter 9, which is partly based on his work. David Ward at Refugee HA commented on government policy aspects of the draft and Myron Hinds (also Refugee HA) on aspects of support plans. Sue Lukes checked legal aspects of the text and drafted various additions. Fidelma O'Hagan commented on Northern Ireland legal issues. Several people such as Sam Lister, Naomi Cohen, Rhys Evans and Merron Simpson helpfully read and commented on draft material. Niki Walton checked the practical examples.

Both hact and the Federation of Black Housing Organisations contributed directly to the guide through pieces of survey work. Discussions on refugee community organisations with Azim El-Hassan and Maknun Gameldin-Ashami (hact associates) were especially useful. Thanks are also due to the RCOs who responded to our survey, joined our discussions or otherwise contributed. ICAR (the Information Centre about Asylum and Refugees) also provided invaluable material.

At government level, various contacts in the Home Office, Scottish Executive, Communities Scotland and the Welsh Assembly Government supplied comments, especially Sam Waugh (seconded to the Home Office/ODPM). Jon Rouse at the Housing Corporation readily agreed to do the Foreword and is personally committed to this area of work.

Well over one hundred practical examples and other suggestions were sent to CIH for the guide, and thanks are due to all those who did so. Special thanks go to those who organised case study visits – Ann Branson and Mani Akyigyina (Leicester), Bel Gallup (Sheffield), Brian O'Hara, Peter Barry and Lynne Carr (Glasgow) and Teresa Carroll (Coventry) – together with the organisations who gave time for interviews or arranged meetings with refugees. I left all of these discussions with a strong impression of the dedication and enthusiasm of those involved.

John Perry
September 2005

GLOSSARY OF ABBREVIATIONS

CHAPTER 1

ABOUT THE GUIDE

❏ What is the purpose of the guide?

This guide will help housing professionals face the challenge of meeting the housing and related needs of asylum seekers and refugees. Some of the material will also be relevant to new migrants more generally – including people coming to Britain from other parts of Europe.

The guide aims to show how safe and secure housing can be provided, and how it can be the crucial link in helping people establish themselves in communities where they want to live and where other people accept them. Good housing services can be the basis for the wider support which new migrants are likely to need. Housing professionals are well-placed to establish partnerships with other organisations which can provide it.

The guide argues that one of the best ways of doing this is to involve refugees and other new migrant groups in assessing the need for, providing and monitoring services.

In focussing on the needs of new migrants, the guide does not ignore the needs of existing communities. Only if their needs are also taken into account will newcomers be accepted. The guide considers how this can be done and how it fits with wider efforts to promote 'community cohesion'.

The term 'new migrants' is used throughout the guide, partly to emphasise the point that housing needs are changing and that many places have new minority ethnic or immigrant communities that have only developed in the past few years. Asylum seekers and refugees coming to Britain are the biggest reason for this change, but not the only one – there are also new groups of economic migrants from other European countries, or secondary migration of refugees accepted elsewhere in Europe. However, there is far less professional expertise and fewer practical examples on these wider issues, so the guide does not aim to cover fully the needs of these groups. It does, however, give the legal entitlements to help on housing issues for all types of migrant.

❑ Who is it for?

The guide is aimed at housing professionals working in local authorities, housing associations and the independent sector. It is directed both at the strategic level and at those responsible for devising and delivering housing and support services. It should also be useful to refugee community organisations and to those responsible for training and development on housing, housing support and asylum and refugee issues.

The guide is aimed particularly at organisations which are starting out in this field or have had some involvement but want to extend the services they provide. Whenever possible, practical examples are used to illustrate the variety and types of services already available.

The guide does not start from the viewpoint that housing providers should meet all the different needs that new migrants may have. Rather, housing is considered to be an appropriate 'way in' to identifying, assessing and helping meet those needs. Housing professionals are able to take a strategic and coordinating role (where appropriate), to provide accommodation and housing-related services, and to help set up the partnerships needed to address wider needs.

The legislation about asylum seekers and refugees is generally UK-wide, and the guide aims to be relevant to and draw examples from all parts of the UK. The guide does not give detailed guidance on the legislation, except for the relationship between immigration and housing law (homelessness, housing benefit and the letting of permanent accommodation) on which there are details in appendices 2 and 3.

Readers should bear in mind that this is a policy area in which changes frequently occur. Details in the guide may therefore become out-of-date. However, the principles and practical advice are intended to be longer-lasting.

❑ How was the guide compiled?

The main text of the guide is partly based on published sources such as research reports or drawn from detailed good practice guidance on particular services for new migrants (such as interpreter services). Rather than clutter the text, most references are given in appendix 1. Other advice has come from discussions with practitioners who are already providing services, with researchers who have examined these issues in more detail than has been possible in the guide, and with refugees and refugee organisations.

Almost 50 practical examples have been included to show how housing and other organisations have responded to the needs of new migrants in different parts of the UK. These have largely been supplied by the organisations themselves, and most will welcome contact from readers who want more details. To avoid material getting out of date, where possible references are made to websites or other ways of obtaining further information rather than giving contact names or personal phone numbers.

The guide does not identify the practical examples as 'good practice', because of the difficulty of evaluating them individually. They are sources of ideas or promising approaches – rather than examples of how ideally things should be done. Appendix 5 gives more detail on how the examples were compiled and a table sets out some of the characteristics of the examples and how they were verified.

However the guide *does* recommend or set out 'good practice' in a broader sense, in the main body of the text. These 'good practice' points are derived either from the established literature on the subject, or by reference to other guidance (eg on local housing strategies) which can be applied to the subject of asylum seekers and refugees.

❑ How is the guide organised?

Chapter 2 says why housing issues are important, defines terms and gives basic facts. Chapter 3 looks in more detail at the people the guide is considering, their needs and the ways in which they enter Britain and settle here.

Chapters 4, 5 and 6 are about how to go about meeting these needs. Accommodation is looked at first, then building a new life (which considers issues like support needs in the home, learning English and getting a job), and finally the issues about living in a community. Each topic is dealt with in two sections in each chapter, the first covering the policy and giving good practice advice, the second containing the practical examples collected for the guide.

The next three chapters deal with strategic issues. Chapter 7 is about the partnerships likely to be necessary, at local, regional and national levels, to provide effective services. Chapter 8 is about resources – finance, skills and information. Chapter 9 shows how to go about drawing up a refugee housing strategy for your organisation or area, taking account of the issues in all the preceding chapters.

Appendices give references to material mentioned in the text, set out legislation relating to immigration and housing, provide the context of national policy on immigration and how it is developing, describe how practical examples were collected, give contact details for national organisations and list key reports and publications.

CHAPTER 2

THE CHALLENGE FOR
HOUSING ORGANISATIONS

What this chapter is about

- why housing professionals face a particular challenge
- defining the terms – asylum seekers, refugees and new migrants
- migration, asylum seekers and refugees – basic facts

Britain's population has always been added to by people coming from abroad, and it goes without saying that their first priority is likely to be a safe and secure place in which to live.

Significant numbers of people still come to live in Britain from places such as the Caribbean and India and Pakistan, which have long-established communities in many British towns and cities. But increasingly, migration to Britain is more diverse and more affected by political events elsewhere. People from countries like Iraq, Somalia and Zimbabwe are now coming here in bigger numbers than before, often because of war or other major problems. Many of these newcomers will seek asylum when they arrive here. Other 'new' migrant groups may arrive for different political, economic or social reasons. For example, the expansion of the EU makes it possible for people from east European countries to look for jobs in Britain.

These changes in who wants to live here pose a challenge, both to British society and, more specifically, to housing organisations. The challenge to society in the broadest sense is how to accept these newcomers. It is a debate which is reflected almost every day in the news media and what is said in parliament. For local communities, there is the challenge of responding to people who may come from places with which they are unfamiliar, and from which there are few people already living here who might help them. Even worse, new migrants may be branded as 'illegals' or otherwise treated as not deserving help. And events in London in summer 2005 make it even more important that successful integration and community cohesion are high on the agenda of all organisations working in this field.

❏ The importance of housing

For housing professionals, there is a more specific challenge: how to provide newcomers with secure and safe accommodation, and how to support them while they are in it. If they are asylum seekers, they may only be eligible for limited help, channelled in specific ways. Once their right to stay here is established, their need for longer-term accommodation may be very urgent. Many of the people concerned will not initially speak English and may be badly affected by what has happened to them in their home country or on the way here. Already, there are indications that growing numbers of people who are sleeping rough or are in temporary accommodation came here to seek asylum, but for one reason or another have fallen through the safety net.

Yet as a Home Office research report about refugees has said:

> '*Housing plays a key role in refugees' long-term resettlement. Without decent housing, or at least a roof over their heads, refugees find it extremely difficult to rebuild their lives. Housing can provide safety, security and stability to people who feel they have lost everything in their flight to safety.*' Carey-Wood, J (1997)

Although there are some excellent practical examples of services to asylum seekers and refugees, there is also wide recognition that housing providers have failed to engage with these needs to the extent required. This was acknowledged by the Chief Executive of the Housing Corporation when he said (24 June 2004) that 'we and housing associations generally have not pulled our weight' in serving the needs of refugees and asylum seekers. He also criticised local authorities for failing to consider refugee housing in their strategic planning. National organisations such as CIH and NHF have made similar criticisms.

Some housing organisations may consider that this issue is not relevant to them as they do not operate in one of the main conurbations or in a port of entry to the UK, or do not have an established refugee community. However, many organisations in similar circumstances *do* engage with the issue, suggesting that both the need and the capacity exist. The government's policy towards asylum seekers also has widespread effects. For example, the private sector may be accommodating asylum seekers in an area under a government contract, creating a need for services to support those asylum seekers or to step in if the arrangement with the private landlord breaks down.

As the guide will show, the myths and adverse publicity in the press cannot disguise the fact that many people arriving in the UK to claim asylum are escaping severe persecution or even torture, and have endured considerable hardship to get here. Not only does this demand a humanitarian response, but it often makes their needs and circumstances quite different from those of – for example – the established BME communities that have existed for many decades. This has to be borne strongly in mind in developing appropriate services.

> *'They say to me, you should close your mouth, and if you don't close your mouth we will cut off your tongue.'*
>
> Yusif, Iraqi Kurd asylum seeker, The Guardian (2001) *Welcome to Britain.*

This guide aims to help all those who want to respond to the challenge of providing better housing and related services for asylum seekers, refugees and new migrants more generally – especially in places where services do not exist or fall short of what is needed.

❑ Asylum seekers, refugees and new migrants – definitions

Immigration law is very complex: there are different kinds of status for people who have a right to stay in Britain, people's status can change, and the law is constantly being modified. The law itself is partly what is in acts of parliament, partly what is decided by the courts, and partly international law. The press complicates matters by wrongly referring to people (for example) as 'illegal asylum seekers' when in fact anyone has the right to come to Britain and seek asylum.

To simplify matters, the guide uses the following terms. None of these definitions is technical:

- *asylum* is the protection under United Nations conventions, given by one country to people from another, who are often fleeing persecution, torture or war
- *asylum seekers* are people who have applied for asylum, but whose cases have not yet been decided or are subject to legal appeal
- the *point of decision* is the point at which asylum seekers are notified of the outcome of their application, and the period (currently 28 days) following that when the initial support they received as asylum seekers ends
- *refugees* are people whose application for asylum has been accepted. A person with refugee status will be granted leave to stay in Britain and have rights to housing, to work, and many of the other rights of full citizens (more detail on the different kinds of refugee status is in chapter 3)
- *people refused asylum* are those whose applications have been rejected, but are still living here either because they are awaiting return to their home country or have decided to stay without permission
- *new migrants* is the term used (in this sense, specific to the guide) to refer broadly to people who have come to live in Britain for whatever reason, including economic and social reasons as well as those seeking asylum, especially from countries which do not already have large, established communities here
- *long-term residents* are people established in Britain and forming the 'host' communities for new migrants – who may themselves be from minority ethnic groups.

The guide focuses especially on asylum seekers and refugees, but will have some relevance to all of the categories of people just described.

❏ Migration, asylum seekers and refugees – some basic facts

So much is said about the numbers of people coming into the UK, and particularly about people seeking asylum, that it is important to establish some basic facts.

Britain's population is now about 60 million, and is expected to grow to about 64m by 2030, before starting to fall. Migration is an important element: each year, between 150,000 and 200,000 extra people come to live in to the UK, compared with natural population increases of little more than 50,000. As migrants are generally younger than existing residents, they help to slow the shift towards an ageing population.

One in twelve people now living in Britain was born overseas. More than half of these are from the US or 'old Commonwealth' countries like Canada and Australia, and the other major groups are people from the Indian sub-continent and other 'new Commonwealth countries'.

Asylum seekers are not included in these figures until they are accepted for settlement. There are now about 40,000 asylum seekers (including dependants) arriving annually, down from 100,000 in 2002. Many other European countries receive proportionally more asylum seekers than Britain, relative to their population size.

In 2004 about 54,000 people were accepted as refugees and allowed to stay on a long-term basis in the UK. In the last few years this figure has usually been between 10-40,000 people each year. But in the early 1990s acceptances were much lower. Recent higher numbers reflect the government's attempts to deal with the backlog of asylum cases, and the recent peak in applications. In all probability acceptances will soon fall back to previous levels. In 2004, about one in every seven people accepted for UK residence came originally as asylum seekers.

Behind the headline figures about numbers of new arrivals is a less-than-complete picture of who is here and where they are. Currently (2005) there are just over 60,000 asylum seekers in the UK supported by the National Asylum Support Service (NASS). Two-thirds of these receive accommodation, and one-third just receive subsistence help. What is not known are the numbers now here who refused NASS help in the first place, or have not secured refugee status but are still here unknown to NASS. Probably numbering many thousands, these people are particularly vulnerable.

Where NASS provides accommodation, this is generally outside London, following the government's policy of 'dispersal' (see chapter 3). More than three-quarters of asylum seekers housed through NASS are in the Midlands, the north of England, Wales or Scotland (see figure 2.1). However, of those only receiving subsistence, the opposite is true: three-quarters are living in London and the south-east. A recent assessment put the total numbers of asylum seekers in London at 43,000 (end of 2004).

Figure 2.1: Dispersal of asylum seekers accommodated by NASS

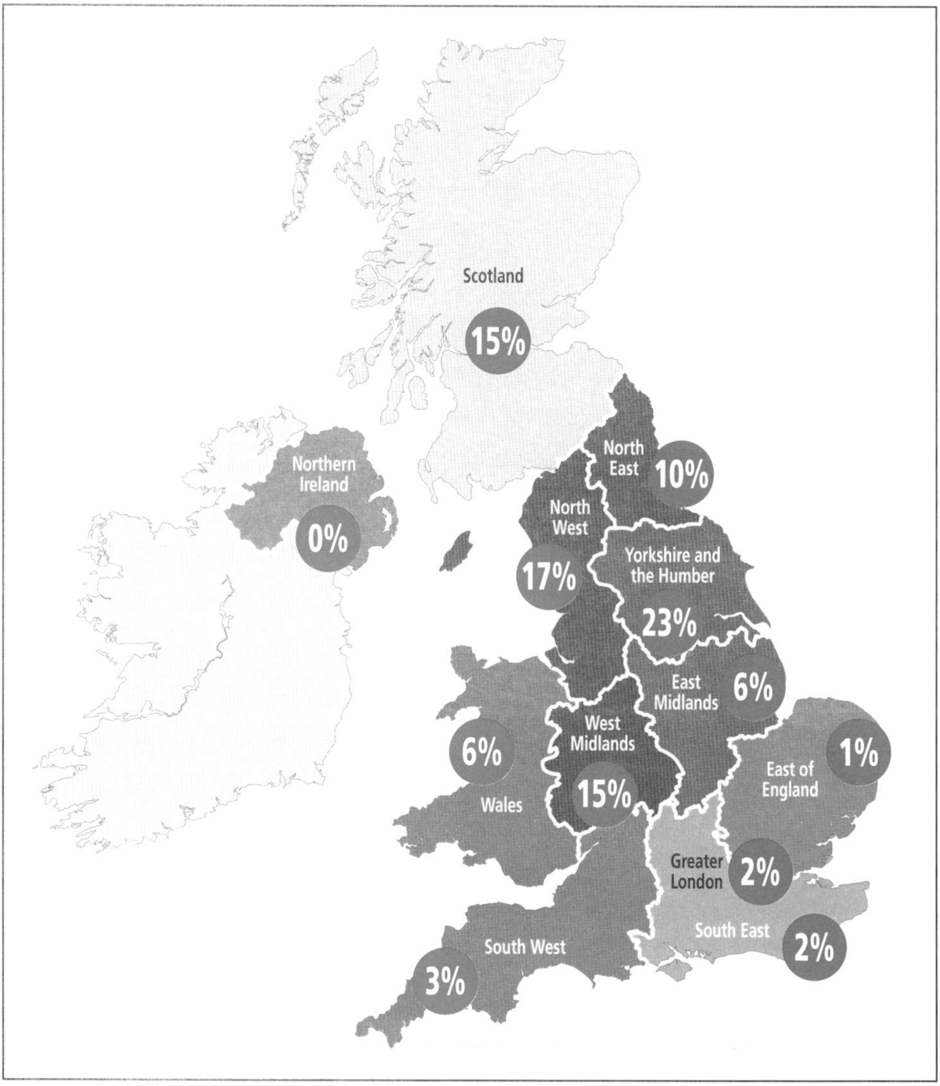

Source: Home Office Asylum Statistics 1st Quarter 2005
Note: there are currently (June, 2005) 120 asylum seekers accommodated by NASS in Northern Ireland, but not under the dispersal scheme.

As explained above, each year several thousand people are accepted as refugees. For those leaving NASS accommodation, local authorities can establish information-sharing protocols that will help to identify their needs. But for other accepted refugees, information about them and where they live is more difficult to obtain, although 'snapshots' are provided by the census and other surveys. Local needs surveys (dealt with in chapter 9) are therefore much more likely than national figures to help in identifying people in these groups.

As well as asylum seekers and refugees, other new migrants may have similar needs. For example, many recent Somali arrivals in fact came from other European countries like Holland, and are not counted in asylum or refugee statistics. Groups like these can only be identified through local surveys.

Checklist on overall issues

- ✓ find out whether asylum seekers are accommodated in the area where your organisation works
- ✓ find out who is providing housing and related services
- ✓ question whether the extent of migration is known in your area, and whether information is available on who is coming from where
- ✓ ask whether there is any evidence (for example, through rough sleeping or begging) of new migrants falling through the 'safety net' and not having sufficient support
- ✓ find out whether there is anyone 'in charge' of these issues locally (someone responsible for getting the information and looking at the implications for local services)

CHAPTER 3

PEOPLE AND THEIR NEEDS

What this chapter is about

- characteristics of asylum seekers and new migrants
- needs they are likely to have
- the process by which people enter Britain as asylum seekers
- the decision-making process
- the support which people are entitled to while awaiting a decision
- other routes by which refugees come to Britain

Asylum seekers and refugees are likely to be different from the resident population in many different ways, some obvious and others less so. Their accommodation needs will also be different and will vary according to the stage that their asylum application has reached. All new migrants are likely to have a range of wider needs, but particularly so those people who are seeking asylum from repressive regimes or who are divided from their families.

This chapter is about the people who are the subject of this guide, their needs, and the ways that they are dealt with by the official systems when they come to the UK. It sets the scene for the following three chapters which look in more detail at these needs, how they are met, and the role of housing agencies. This chapter focuses particularly on the two key stages that asylum seekers pass through – their arrival in the UK, and the 'point of decision' on their refugee status and whether they can remain.

> 'Successful integration begins on the day people arrive, not the day they get refugee status.'
>
> hact (2004), response to *Integration Matters*.

❑ Who are they and where do they come from?

Much of what is known about asylum seekers and refugees comes from the information collected at the time their application is made, usually shortly after their arrival. Beyond that stage, information is less complete and less reliable although various research projects are helping to improve the picture.

Where do asylum seekers come from?
Currently (2005) the highest numbers of asylum seekers are coming from Iran, Iraq, Somalia, China, and the Democratic Republic of Congo. These patterns change though as conditions in different countries change.

Who are they?
A typical asylum seeker is young (under 35), more likely to be male than female and unlikely to have family dependants with him or her. In 2004, just under 34,000 applicants had only just over 6,000 family members with them. Over two-thirds of asylum seekers were male, and over three-quarters were under 35 years old. (This picture may be different in the dispersal areas, where there is a greater proportion of families.)

What about their children?
Most asylum seekers have no children with them. Many have left families behind – who are likely to want them to join them if they get accepted as refugees. Some asylum seekers are children travelling independently. Since 2000, about 15,000 unaccompanied asylum-seeking children (UASC) have entered Britain, the big majority being 14-17 year olds.

Is enough information available to judge accommodation needs?
Other than knowing about children and the very small proportion of older people, little more is known about the characteristics of asylum seekers that might be useful to housing organisations. For example, if asylum seekers bring families or elderly relatives after their cases have been decided, they do not feature in the statistics. So the need for large family accommodation or for accommodation accessible to disabled people is not apparent in national figures and can only be established locally.

What languages do they speak?
Information on languages spoken by asylum seekers receiving official support is not published nationally but is available to local authorities in areas of 'dispersal' (see below). So for example in Leicester there are 52 known languages, of which twelve are 'agreed' for the dispersal programme. However, in London boroughs and other places to which asylum seekers go who are not 'dispersed', there is no available language information unless it is collected by (for example) the education authority from its schools.

And other new migrants?
If information on asylum seekers is sparse, that on refugees or other new migrants is even sparser. In 2004, over 140,000 people were given permission to settle permanently in the UK. About 37 percent – 54,000 – were refugees or their dependants. Just under half of these refugees came from Africa and the next

biggest groups were those from Europe and from Asia (other than India). Again, only local surveys are likely to provide any detailed information on people in these categories. One factor to be borne in mind is that people counted as EU nationals in immigration statistics may have been refugees or immigrants from other countries before they became EU citizens (examples are former refugees from Somalia; and migrant workers from countries like Portugal, who may originally be from places like Angola or Mozambique).

Figure 3.1: Reasons for settlement in the UK, 2004

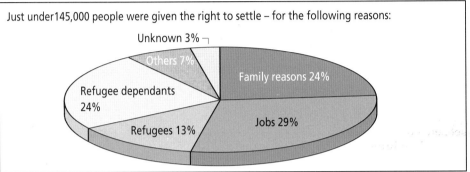

Source: Home Office (2005) *Control of Immigration: Statistics UK 2004.*

Chapter 9 looks at how housing organisations can build up their own more detailed picture of the characteristics of asylum seekers, refugees and new migrants generally, in the areas they serve.

❑ The needs of newcomers to the UK

The starting point for this guide is the need for good, secure accommodation, but housing professionals are well aware that this is not enough in itself. All housing bodies will want to ensure that new tenants can make proper use of the accommodation, that it is in an appropriate area, and that tenants receive the support they need to keep their tenancy – that it is 'sustainable' in many different ways. Some housing agencies will want to go beyond this to provide – or at least secure the availability of – the wider services that are particularly needed by this client group.

What follows is a snapshot of typical needs. Following chapters consider these in more detail.

■ Accommodation

Most accommodation for asylum seekers is provided through the NASS dispersal programme, or in the private sector. Refugees and other new migrants with 'leave to remain' in Britain (see box, page 17) are eligible for housing in the normal way.

Particularly important for the purposes of this guide is the point of decision when an asylum seeker finds out if he/she is an accepted refugee, and has only a very short time in which to secure permanent accommodation.

Accommodation needs are dealt with in chapter 4.

Housing-related needs

People who are newly-arrived in the country or have moved into permanent accommodation from a hostel are likely to need support with very practical issues about using their accommodation. Some of this will be the same as for any new tenant (running the heating system) but some may be much more basic (changing a light bulb or using a cooker).

Asylum seekers have little or no spare cash so accepted refugees may start their tenancy with none of the basics like a cooker, fridge or furniture.

Accepted refuges and other new migrants entitled to benefits will need help in applying for housing benefit, income support, etc. They may need more general help in dealing with correspondence and paperwork.

Immediate wider needs

Unfamiliarity with things that people here take for granted does not just apply in the home but to the wider world. Schools and other local services, dentists, the postal system, telephones are all likely to be unfamiliar, particularly to new arrivals. Limited resources make it difficult for asylum seekers, especially, to travel or to use leisure facilities.

> *'Never assume that the refugee has the knowledge about something. Advice on even the smallest things which we don't think are that serious could be a big help, eg explaining how the system of buses runs in his/her area ...'*
> Dash Koci, refugee working for Accord HA

Language
Although many asylum seekers speak English most do not. Even if one member of the family is English speaking, others may not be. Access to services via someone who speaks the same language is vitally important. Many agencies experienced in this field emphasise the communication difficulties that arise in interviewing refugees – and not only because of the language barrier (see chapter 4).

Schools
Children of asylum seekers and refugees enter the education system in the same way as children of long-standing residents, but parents may need help in liaising with schools and making sure children feel accepted.

Health and wellbeing

People need access to a GP and a dentist, and advice on how to use those services. Many asylum seekers have been traumatised by torture or imprisonment and may need specialist help. Many more are likely to be suffering stress or anxiety for more general reasons like separation from their home environment and often from their family. Others may have physical impairments affecting their accommodation needs.

Legal and immigration advice

Asylum seekers need legal advice and advocacy in order to pursue their claims or challenge adverse decisions, and accepted refugees may want to bring other family members to Britain or get advice on citizenship. Free services are needed – or ones accessible through legal aid. Many people (eg those coming from dictatorial regimes) do not realise they have access to legal help and are able to challenge administrative decisions.

Longer-term needs

Accepted refugees looking to build a new life in Britain will want to develop their English, possibly receive further training and find employment.

Training

Asylum seekers may be able to undertake courses (eg English for speakers of other languages – ESOL) and refugees and other new migrants may also want to pursue work-related or other forms of training.

Employment

Getting a job is likely to be a priority for accepted refugees and new migrants generally, including possibly adapting an existing qualification so that it can be used here.

These three types of support needs are dealt with in chapter 5.

■ Community-related needs

A central theme of this guide is the importance of measures to help new migrants to be accepted in the neighbourhoods where they are living, and the work this may require with long-term residents.

Housing professionals should be aware that just as 'minority ethnic groups' do not necessarily share the same needs, attitudes or goals, newer migrant groups may be even more diverse and may have many cultural differences with established ethnic minority people in the community. Refugees may have similar cultural backgrounds but be from different 'sides' in the conflict from which they have escaped. And of course, the needs of women, of children, of older people and disabled people will all require consideration.

Relating to other refugees

Many of the people who are the subject of this guide may want to establish contact – if they have not done so already – with other people from the same country or who speak the same language. Some of the support they need can then be drawn from these contacts and relationships. Making these links can be an important factor in where they want to live. Some refugees will want to practice religious faiths – facilities may be lacking, or not welcoming to particular groups.

Relating to the wider community

This is a wide-ranging topic which is discussed later in more detail. It extends from the need to be accepted (or, at least, not rejected) by neighbours, including tackling issues like anti-social behaviour and racist harassment, to making more positive moves towards integration with the community and 'community cohesion'. At a strategic level, there are issues such as portrayal of new migrants in the local media, relations with the police, provision for new religious groups, and many others, in which housing professionals may to some extent be involved.

Community-related needs are dealt with in chapter 6.

❏ The asylum process

There are two key stages in the process by which someone enters the UK to obtain asylum: the point of entry, and the point of decision on their right to stay. What follows is a basic guide to this process, not a statement of the law. Sources which provide detailed information on the legal and administrative systems are given in appendix 6.

■ Entering Britain as an asylum seeker

People who enter Britain to seek asylum may do so conventionally (eg arriving by air, perhaps as a visitor) or otherwise. Some people – possibly women and children – may have been trafficked into Britain against their will.

People may apply for asylum either at the 'port of entry' or once they have entered the country. These 'in country' applications have to be made at the immigration service at Croydon or one of the public enquiry offices (Birmingham, Glasgow or Liverpool – or in Northern Ireland, at Belfast International Airport).

The asylum decision-making process which then begins is described in figure 3.2 overleaf.

After initial screening, an asylum applicant is likely to be released into the UK while his/her application is dealt with. (The guide does not cover the issue of people held in detention centres.) Decisions on asylum applications used to take several months but progress is now being made towards the target of making them within two months.

Figure 3.2: Decision-making process and support arrangements for newly-arriving asylum seekers

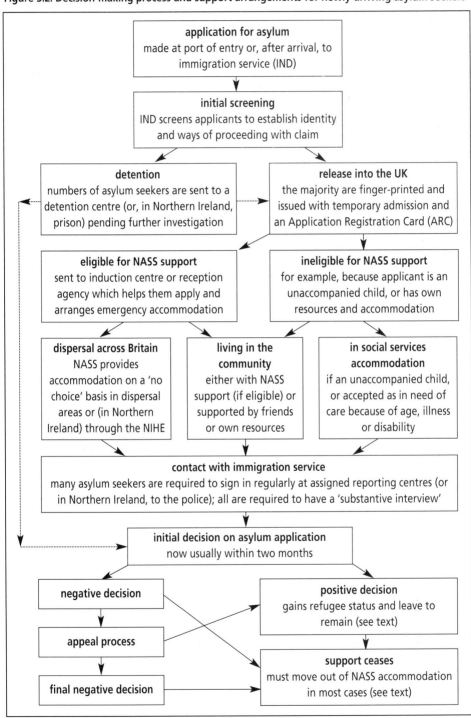

Source: adapted from hact (2003), p13.

■ Entitlement to accommodation and wider support

Most asylum seekers are not eligible for local authority housing, but can get accommodation through certain defined routes (see chapter 4). Neither are asylum seekers entitled to any other state benefits, only very limited support through vouchers exchangeable for cash at post offices. They are however entitled to some wider services such as health care, schools and police protection. They are not usually allowed to do paid work, but may take part in some training (including learning English).

While awaiting a decision on their application, asylum seekers may have to report to the immigration service (the Immigration and Nationality Directorate of the Home Office, or 'IND') or in Northern Ireland, to the police. They will also have a 'substantive interview' to enable the immigration service to assess their case.

■ Decisions on asylum cases

A positive decision gives the asylum seeker refugee status, or a lesser form of 'leave to remain' in the UK (see box). A negative decision (refusal of the asylum application) may be the subject of an appeal.

Different rights to remain

Refugee status means that a person is accepted by the immigration service as suffering persecution in their country of origin and so has been granted asylum. Refugees currently get *indefinite leave to remain* and the right to stay here as long as they wish, having many of the rights of British citizens (although *citizenship* status has to be applied for separately, after five years residence). Refugee status brings with it full rights to live, work, claim benefits and have access to social housing, as well as entitlement to grants and domestic fees for students, and a right to family reunion.

Indefinite leave to remain (ILR) is also known as 'settlement' and is granted to certain migrants after a prescribed period. It also brings with it full rights to live, work, claim benefits and have access to social housing, and an entitlement to grants and domestic fees for students. From 30 August 2005 ILR will no longer be awarded immediately to those who have refugee status: initially they will be given limited leave to remain for five years which will then be subject to review, when they may get ILR. Because they are refugees, this will not affect their rights to work, benefits, etc.

There are three more limited forms of 'leave to remain' which also give access to benefits, local authority housing, etc.

→

They are:

- *Exceptional leave to remain (ELR)* is a form of discretionary permission to be in the UK which is granted to people who do not qualify for refugee status or have any other legal rights to be in the UK. Asylum applicants granted ELR have the right to work and claim benefits and are eligible for local authority housing, but do not have the right to family reunion which refugees have. From 2003, ELR was replaced in the asylum system by two other types of exceptional leave (see below) but may still be granted outside the asylum rules, for other types of migrant.

- *Humanitarian protection (HP)* is granted for up to three years, when the case is reviewed and protection may be extended. It applies to people refused full refugee status but who cannot be returned to their home country because they would be at risk: for example, through adverse conditions caused by war or natural disaster.

- *Discretionary leave (DL)* is a further more restricted category applying to people not covered by the other categories but where there are still compelling reasons why they should not be removed.

Neither HP nor DL status provides rights of family reunion, but it will normally be awarded to all family members who are in the UK with the applicant.

■ What happens to people whose applications are refused?

People refused refugee status or other leave to remain (or who have exhausted the appeals process) are supposed to leave the UK. At this point, one of several things might happen:

- they apply for judicial review of their case
- they show an intention to leave the UK (eg by starting to obtain travel documents)
- the immigration service accepts that they cannot immediately leave the UK, eg because of illness or pregnancy, or because their home country is unsafe, or
- they stay in the UK without permission and with no intention to leave, at which point public support either ends or is available only in certain limited circumstances (eg families with children).

In the first three instances people who are childfree can apply for 'hard case support'. This is only available to people who are now destitute and were previously supported by NASS (or by a local authority under the 'interim arrangements' – see page 27). Support consists either of full-board accommodation, or accommodation supplemented by vouchers for food and drink (the voucher scheme – which has replaced cash payments – has been criticised by a number of agencies). Families with children may be able to stay in NASS accommodation though this may be withdrawn in certain circumstances.

People who stay without permission are frequently dependent on charity in some form – see page 35.

❑ Other ways in which refugees may enter Britain

Applying individually as an asylum seeker, whether at port of entry or 'in country', is the main way by which potential refugees enter the UK. But there are also other ways by which refugees may be 'resettled' in Britain direct from the countries where they are staying as refugees. Some of these routes are described below. (*Resettlement* is the organised movement of selected refugees from their country of first asylum to another country for permanent settlement and integration. It is a specialised protection process for recognised refugees.)

Mandate refugees
Someone may be accepted as a refugee (eg at a refugee camp in or near their country of origin) by the United Nations High Commissioner for Refugees (UNHCR), and apply to come to the UK. Cases are considered on their merits (eg family connection with the UK) and if approved the person is known as a 'mandate refugee' and travels individually to Britain.

The Ten or More programme
This is a programme for resettling disabled refugees. For example, Refugee Housing Association (RHA) works with the Red Cross and UNHCR to receive refugees with an impairment or medical condition, untreatable in their present country of asylum. If the refugee is accepted and comes to the UK, RHA provides intensive support through its supported accommodation service (RHA contact details are in appendix 6).

The Gateway Protection Programme
Refugees have started coming to the UK through this programme which accepts up to 500 refugees each year, nominated by UNHCR. Initially the scheme applied only to refugees in West Africa, and they were resettled in places such as Sheffield and Bolton. Safe Haven Yorkshire are housing, and RHA are supporting, 20 refugees in three areas of Sheffield who arrived direct from West Africa under the Gateway programme. Accommodation is provided by the city council's ALMO (Sheffield Homes), South Yorkshire HA and Yorkshire Housing Group (further details: Inside Housing, 5 November 2004, pp18-21). The scheme has recently extended to refugees from Myanmar/Burma.

An informal route by which refugees come to Britain is from other European countries where they have previously had refugee status but are now (usually) citizens. An example is the growth of the Somali population in cities such as Leicester, mainly due to migration from countries such as the Netherlands. Although not classed as refugees for immigration purposes, they have many similar needs to refugees arriving through formal routes and are legally able to settle because as EU nationals they have freedom of movement.

Checklist on people and their needs

✓ find out what information is available on asylum seekers, refugees and other new migrant groups in your area

✓ consider initiating surveys to obtain this information (eg through local social housing providers or through refugee community organisations)

✓ look at the checklist of housing and other needs and consider how it applies in your area, and whether the needs are being met

✓ make sure that at least one responsible person in your organisation is familiar with the asylum and refugee decision-making process, and the rules about accommodation and support

✓ consider whether your organisation could engage with one of the programmes for receiving accepted refugees into Britain

CHAPTER 4

A PLACE TO LIVE

What this chapter is about

- why housing is important
- asylum seekers, refugees and new migrants as 'customers'
- providing information and advice on housing options
- the kinds of accommodation that might be available
- housing in different sectors
- rough sleeping and destitution
- practical examples of accommodation projects and services

It is hardly necessary to emphasise the value to everyone of having secure accommodation, but in the case of new migrants it is particularly important for a number of reasons. First, in the case of asylum seekers, it is a chance to obtain some security after, perhaps, weeks of travelling, of separation from family and friends, and – often – real personal danger. Second, for refugees and other new migrants, housing may be the first step to building a new life. Third, having a secure place to live – apart from being important in itself – means that other family members might be able to come to the UK. Fourth, it provides an address – allowing benefits to be claimed and jobs to be applied for. Finally, it gives access to wider services such as schools and health care.

As research commissioned by the Home Office pointed out:

> '*As a result of refugees' fears of hostility and their language difficulties, childcare commitments, unemployment and low incomes, many of them will spend a large proportion of their time in their own homes; therefore the quality and appropriateness of their accommodation is particularly significant for them.*' Carey-Wood, J (1997)

This chapter is about access to good quality accommodation in the right location – a secure roof over the head of the asylum seeker, refugee or new migrant. The first section describes policy and advises on good practice. The second gives detailed practical examples.

'*Housing is the key to the door of integration.*'
Heather Petch, hact, *Housing Today*, 22 October 2004

Section 1: Policy and Good Practice Guidance

❏ Asylum seekers, refugees and new migrants as 'customers'

Most housing practitioners are used to helping people in housing need. But they may not be familiar with the particular requirements of assisting the people who are the subject of this guide. It should not be assumed that staff who are from minority ethnic groups, or have experience of BME customers, will necessarily know the problems, needs and difficulties of new migrants (this is one reason for recruiting from new migrant groups, and for staff training, dealt with in chapter 8.) Lack of a common language is also an obvious barrier to communication.

Finding or being allocated accommodation can be even more stressful for new migrants than for other applicants. Possible symptoms of this stress have been identified as poor timekeeping for appointments, poor ability to concentrate (eg during interviews), lack of motivation and poor self-esteem (eg not expressing views on the suitability or otherwise of accommodation offered.)

Obviously, in discussing family circumstances and needs, issues about the reasons for the customer coming to the UK, and for their possible separation from their families, are bound to arise. This requires considerable sensitivity on the part of the interviewer and the ability and patience to gain the interviewee's confidence. While it is necessary to obtain information, it is also important to avoid giving the impression that the interviewee's motives are being questioned, or to probe unnecessarily for details of persecution they may have suffered. Questions such as 'why did you come to the UK?' should be avoided.

Experienced workers in this field point out that one of the most important things is to listen respectfully to peoples' explanations of why they are here. Staff themselves often fail to realise how important this is or may think they are 'wasting their time'. It is useful to reassure frontline staff that this is not the case.

One difficulty that housing practitioners may face is that new migrants may come from places and situations in which people in authority were threatening and confidentiality was by no means guaranteed. Also in some circumstances local authorities may have to contact the Home Office to ask about a person's status. There is also a power for the Home Office to require local authorities to provide information on a specific individual whom they believe to be connected to the area. Detailed advice for housing providers on the legal aspects of interviewing new migrants is in appendix 2.

CIH recommends that all housing professionals avoid putting people in positions where they may compromise their immigration status. Clear information about confidentiality and its limits should be available, and asylum seekers and others whose status is not resolved should be encouraged to seek support and advice from non-statutory and informal services. Liaison with these will ensure that any problems with insensitivity in service delivery that might discourage applicants are identified.

■ When do new migrants become 'customers' of social housing providers?

The apparently simple answer is that new migrants only become 'customers' once their immigration status is decided and they are eligible for housing and other support. However, the real answer is more complex:

- *Housing associations* are not bound by the same restrictions as local authorities, and should in principle treat new migrants as any other applicants (see below). Some asylum seekers or workers on work permits, for example, may be able to pay their rent even though ineligible for housing benefit, so should not be discriminated against.

- *Asylum seekers* may indirectly be customers of local housing authorities or housing associations – even though not secure tenants – because of accommodation contracts with NASS, or arrangements to accommodate young people in the care of social services.

- *Asylum seekers* may receive support services from local authorities or housing associations in NASS accommodation.

- *Longer-established asylum seekers*, still awaiting a decision, may be housed by the local authority (or by another 'out of borough' authority) under the 'interim arrangements' established before NASS became fully operational (see below).

- *Asylum seekers* who are accommodating themselves may seek help at housing advice centres if they lose their accommodation, eg if they are thrown out by friends with whom they were staying.

- *People refused asylum* – and others ineligible for housing – who remain in the UK, including even those with a temporary right to do so, may become destitute and seek help – albeit that the ability of local authorities to help them is restricted.

- *All potential refugees* – including asylum seekers in NASS accommodation – need information and advice *before* the point of decision if their transition to more permanent housing is to be problem-free.

Local authorities are part of government and there are complex rules governing their ability to help new migrants, depending on their immigration status, which vary across the different parts of the UK. However, housing associations, including those created through stock transfer from local authorities, are *not* governed by the same rules and in principle have to treat all applicants equally and not discriminate against anyone because of their immigration status. To do so would open them to challenge under race relations legislation. In practice, though, there is an overlap with the restrictions governing local authorities, in four ways:

- *Nomination agreements.* The ability of housing associations to consider other applicants depends on whether they have lettings that are not subject to nomination agreements. If all their lettings are governed by such agreements, they will have no discretion.
- *Common housing registers or lettings agreements.* These should not inadvertently constrain the associations in the scheme to the same rules that apply to the local authority(ies). Some applicants may be eligible for housing by an association who would not be eligible for council housing.
- *Housing benefit.* Some new migrants are not allowed to receive HB, at least initially (see below, and appendix 3). However, an applicant who fulfils the letting criteria and is able to pay the rent (for example, from wages) should be considered in the same way as any other applicant.
- *Stock transfers.* Particular issues arise, especially with whole stock transfers. Associations should consider carefully how their lettings policies relate to immigration law and not simply follow the previous local authority practice without considering whether as an association they have different legal constraints.

Bearing these distinctions in mind, this chapter now looks in more detail at the two main 'routes' into accommodation and support – as asylum seekers and – following the point of decision – as refugees. It then briefly considers accommodation for other new migrants, and the problem of destitution.

❏ Routes into accommodation and support – asylum seekers

■ Accommodation and support – the process

Asylum seekers may apply for government accommodation and support, and the process is separate from – but linked with – the asylum decision-making procedure described in chapter 3. Accommodation and support arrangements are normally made by NASS. An asylum seeker should apply for NASS support at the time when they make their asylum claim (or later – in some circumstances – see below).

While their application is assessed, asylum seekers may be offered emergency accommodation or may be accommodated in an induction centre. Although housing associations and refugee organisations (for example, the Scottish Refugee Council in Glasgow) provide emergency accommodation, it is also provided in the private sector where appropriate support may not be available. Numbers can be substantial – at the end of 2004 there were 425 people in emergency accommodation in Birmingham and 650 in Manchester – although the national total at 4,650 was one third of what it was two years earlier. People typically stay in emergency accommodation for six months, but those in Glasgow get 'dispersed' accommodation within a few weeks while those in Nottingham wait on average 10 months. In Northern Ireland, the council for ethnic minorities (NICEM) arranges emergency support.

The alternative to emergency accommodation is being sent to an induction centre. These were introduced both to provide initial accommodation and to enable health checks to be made and applicants to receive explanation of their rights and responsibilities in their own language. Currently there are centres in Dover, Leeds and Manchester (more are planned): they housed 615 people at the end of 2004.

The government intended to remove entitlement to support for what were deemed to be late claims for asylum, ie where there is a delay between entry to the country and the claim being made. Under s55 of the Nationality, Immigration & Asylum Act 2002, single, non-disabled asylum seekers aged 18 or over are not entitled to support from NASS (and have no right to appeal) unless they claim asylum 'as soon as reasonably practicable' on arrival. The interpretation of the act was successfully challenged in the courts and there are now very limited circumstances where support can be denied (described, with case examples, in NASS policy bulletin 75 – see appendix 6).

There are many other reasons why NASS may refuse or withdraw support – for example when the asylum seeker is alleged not to be cooperating with immigration officials, has failed to adhere to reporting requirements or is guilty of seriously violent behaviour. There is a right of appeal to the Asylum Support Adjudicators (ASA). There is a shortage of lawyers working in this field – only half of the cases going to the ASA have legal representation and hardly any at the hearing itself. A new service has been established – the Asylum Support Appeals Project – to advise and represent people in these cases (see appendix 6).

■ Accommodation and support – the options

New asylum seekers are normally eligible for one or more of these accommodation or support options:

- *Accommodation and support.* Asylum seekers may apply to NASS for accommodation and support and this is provided on a 'no choice' basis, normally in one of the 'dispersal areas' across England, Scotland and Wales.
- *Subsistence-only support.* Asylum seekers may elect to find their own accommodation and receive subsistence-only support from NASS, which will be through payments made via a post office near to where they live (usually with friends or relatives, and often in London or other big cities).
- *Unaccompanied minors and those with care needs.* Unaccompanied asylum-seeking children (UASC) under 18 are the responsibility of social services. People with care needs do not get NASS support and must be supported by the local authority social services department once they are assessed as needing care due to age, illness, disability or other special reason. Social services help may also be extended to women who are pregnant.
- *Own arrangements.* Asylum seekers with resources or family or friends may provide for themselves.

More details on accommodation and subsistence support provided by NASS are given in Figure 4.1. An ICAR navigation guide is in preparation which will set out the legal background in detail (see appendix 6).

Figure 4.1 Accommodation and support for asylum seekers

Accommodation

Accommodation is provided rent-free by NASS through its contracts with local authorities and other providers, generally in 'dispersal' (or 'cluster') areas (see map on page 8). About half is provided by private landlords and half by 'regional consortia' of local authorities and (in Yorkshire) Safe Haven Yorkshire which is a specialist agency set up by two housing associations (see page 93). Some associations like RHA also manage accommodation on behalf of local authorities. During 2005 NASS is reviewing its accommodation contracts and in some cases scaling them down (see appendix 4).

Practical support

In addition to providing accommodation, NASS contracts with other agencies to provide ongoing practical help to asylum seekers who are in NASS accommodation. Assistance includes helping with access to other services, explaining rights and entitlements, providing local contacts and giving advice on decisions on asylum claims.

Cash support

For a period, asylum seekers were provided with vouchers to be exchanged for goods at certain stores. These vouchers were generally replaced by receipt books in April 2002, enabling users to obtain cash at designated post offices. This method is gradually being replaced by Application Registration Cards which contain details such as name, date of birth and nationality. They are presented at post offices to obtain cash support and are also used to access other services for which asylum seekers are eligible. Subsistence support is roughly based on 70% of basic income support. Pregnant women and families with children under the age of three who are receiving support from NASS are entitled to an additional weekly payment, and a one-off 'maternity grant 'is available for a newly-born child.

In the past, there have been doubts about the quality of privately-provided NASS accommodation, partly because it is only inspected every two years and there are no financial penalties for providing unsuitable accommodation. Some of the normal services to protect private tenants may therefore be relevant (see page 34), alongside NASS inspections.

Problems may occur where NASS wants to move people, possibly because a contract with a private provider is ending. NASS has a policy on this, and there is also independent advice on the process (see www.asylumsupport.org.uk/nasswantmetomove.htm).

NASS has resolved many of the problems of placing people in accommodation but there are still accounts of providers not knowing exact numbers 'until the bus arrives' or being unaware of particular needs (eg people being unable to climb stairs).

Northern Ireland is a separate case as far as asylum support is concerned. It is not a dispersal area but NASS provides accommodation for asylum seekers who enter the province (including those who cross the land border) or who apply 'in country'. Accommodation is provided through the Northern Ireland Housing Executive which obtains it through sub-contracts with a housing association (SHAC) and the private sector. NICEM (see above) provides the support service.

The arrangements just described apply to new cases – those that have started since April 2000 when NASS became operational and the dispersal policy began. There are still many asylum seekers housed and supported by local authorities under previous arrangements, especially the 'interim scheme' which is due to be phased out by March 2006. Some 18,000 people are housed under the scheme in London, but there are also many outside London resulting from 'out of borough' placements.

❏ Routes into accommodation and support – refugees

■ The needs of refugees at the point of decision

> '*For a number of people, relief at receiving a positive decision is immediately tempered by a housing crisis. The numbers affected in this way are increasing...*'
> hact (2003) *Between NASS and a Hard Place.*

As pointed out earlier, refugees have the same rights to housing, housing benefit and other forms of support as British citizens. In most cases they also have the right of family reunion, which means making arrangements to bring other family members to join them.

Once a person is accepted as a refugee he/she has only a very short time in which to arrange accommodation, as any support from NASS is withdrawn after only 28 days. This means that steps should be taken to advise asylum seekers about housing options well before the point of decision.

The '28 day period' at the point of decision

In theory, an accepted refugee receiving accommodation and support from NASS has 28 days at the point of decision in which to obtain more permanent housing, secure housing benefit, obtain furniture, and apply for other benefits. In practice the period is often as short as two weeks because of communication failures or administrative problems. Action is vital at this stage to avoid homelessness and plan a move – possibly on a temporary basis at first – into new accommodation.

Whoever accommodates asylum seekers in an area, it is important that the local housing authority is able to provide them with information on housing options at the point of decision, and can coordinate action within the short time available. The NASS accommodation provider is obliged to make 'move on' advice available to asylum seekers, and of course the local authority has a general obligation to provide advice and assistance to prevent homelessness.

For housing organisations (such as those in Housing Market Renewal Pathfinders) which have surplus stock, retaining refugees in the area may be an important source of new demand, as well as helping to maintain the viability of schools and other local services. Evidence from Glasgow has shown that asylum seekers who do not get good advice at this stage may leave the area. Reasons included incomplete resettlement advice, the short timescale before being required to leave NASS accommodation, and wider community-related issues such as racist harassment, shortage of appropriate housing in the right areas, and lack of jobs or training facilities. Communities Scotland has developed a guide *Providing Information to Refugees: A good practice checklist* which sets out a wide range of information that could be included in a 'welcome pack' and has been sent to all Scottish local authorities.

Another issue at the point of decision is the extent to which the number of 'moves' which a refugee has to make can be minimised. In some areas where there is less pressure on accommodation, it may even be possible for the refugee to continue to occupy the house or flat provided as NASS accommodation (although the rent is usually higher as it is likely to be furnished). However, in many cases a move into temporary accommodation – in a hostel or with friends – may be needed initially.

■ Housing options for refugees

In order to give good advice at the point of decision, housing providers need to know not only about the housing options they provide, but those that are on offer from other agencies or created by refugees themselves.

Figure 4.2 opposite shows the set of 'housing options' judged to be available in one locality. Creating such a diagram can help pinpoint issues; for example, research might be carried out through advice agencies dealing with refugees to discover what numbers of people are using the different 'routes' into housing and what levels of awareness there are both among refugees themselves and within different advice agencies as to the options available. This knowledge can then be used to develop policy – for example, in providing alternative routes to accommodation.

Figure 4.2: Refugees' routes into housing

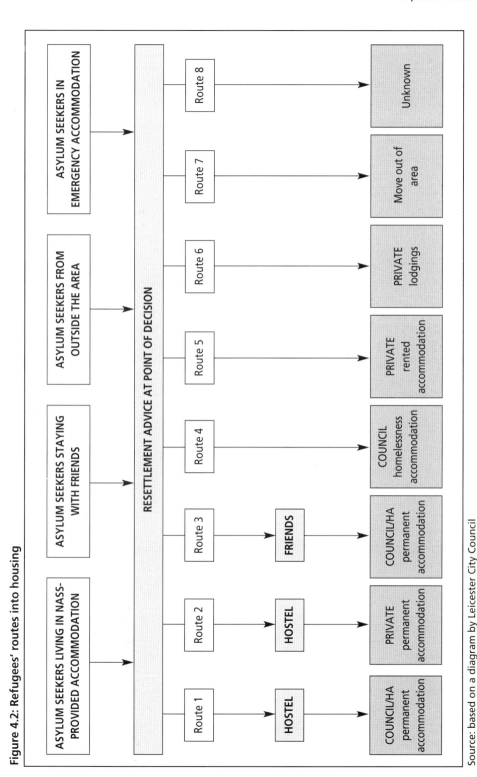

Source: based on a diagram by Leicester City Council

The basic options for refugees at this stage are:

- temporary accommodation (eg in a hostel, or with friends) as a stepping stone to permanent accommodation
- acceptance as being homeless, and being rehoused by the local authority or a housing association
- acceptance on a local housing register and, as a result of having high priority, being permanently rehoused by the local authority or nominated to a housing association
- permanent accommodation (often rented or as lodgings, later possibly as owner-occupiers) in the private sector.

These options are discussed in detail below.

■ The range of housing needs

Some refugees have more complex housing needs. Here are some examples:

Children and young people
Unaccompanied asylum-seeking children (UASC) are the responsibility of social services departments, not NASS. Children up to the age of 16 tend to be accommodated with foster parents or in children's homes. Above that age they may well be in supported accommodation in the private sector (or in some cases, housing associations – RHA provides such accommodation in London). A national register now exists for UASC cases (www.nruc.gov.uk), and Save the Children publishes a guide to rights and entitlements in these cases.

Recent case law has established that social services authorities have the same responsibility to give transitional care to 18 year old asylum seekers or refugees leaving care, as they have to other young people. In Northern Ireland, Barnado's has a project called Leaving Care which supports young people for up to 18 months.

Families
Many 'single' refugees are entitled to bring their immediate family to join them. They may need assistance in this process. For example, Glasgow's Family Reunion Project aims to reunite spouses and children within nine months. The challenge this creates for housing providers is threefold:

- deciding how the original applicant should be housed when he/she receives a positive decision, bearing in mind the probability of family reunion
- how far the arrival of the family can be anticipated, avoiding if possible having to treat them as homeless and placing them in temporary accommodation, perhaps for several months
- in some cases, meeting the need for larger family accommodation that may be in short supply.

Another possible complication is where an asylum seeker gets HP or DL and is then joined by family members who have to go through the asylum system themselves;

during this period they are not eligible for council housing or housing benefit in their own right.

Disabled people

There is no central information on the prevalence of impairments and chronic illness among refugees, although there is some evidence that it is significant. Research shows that the needs of disabled people are often overlooked.

Problems in meeting the needs of disabled refugees

Unmet personal care needs, unsuitable housing and a lack of aids and equipment are common. Other problems include a lack of knowledge about entitlements or how to get a community care assessment, communication difficulties and extreme isolation. Staff dealing with refugees often lack knowledge about disability-related entitlements.

The government's dispersal policy is criticised as insensitive to the needs of disabled people. There is an acute need for better joint working between the different agencies. With few exceptions, relations seem very strained, because of:

- unclear policies and procedures and lack of named contacts equipped to handle enquiries about disabled asylum seekers, especially in NASS

- considerable confusion in and across agencies about responsibilities for financing community care packages and suitable housing

- overstretched social services resources, which sometimes means the needs of disabled refugees and asylum seekers are seen as less pressing than those of other disabled people in the locality.

Source: summarised from Roberts, K and Harris, J (2002).

❏ Refugee housing options in more detail

This section now looks at the four main housing options in more detail. Appendix 3 contains a full schedule of the entitlements to housing, housing benefit and help under homelessness legislation. Readers should consult this for detailed guidance.

■ Temporary accommodation

There are several reasons why temporary accommodation may be needed at the point of decision. First, as pointed out earlier, time is very short, and may well be insufficient to allow allocation of a property on a permanent basis. Second, many refugees are single people who may not be immediately eligible for permanent accommodation. Third, some refugees have housing needs (eg larger family accommodation) that may be difficult to meet quickly. Fourth, single refugees may be planning to bring family members as quickly as possible to the UK and may want temporary accommodation in the meantime.

Whether temporary accommodation is provided by the local authority – for example, in a hostel for homeless people, or a temporary letting – will very much depend on local interpretation of homelessness legislation and whether single refugees (for example) are considered to be 'vulnerable' (see below). Housing associations may have more flexibility. For example, Focus Futures in Birmingham provides emergency access to its hostel schemes for people who are homeless, including refugees.

Alternatively, longer-stay supported accommodation may be available – such as in hostels providing for homeless or vulnerable single people. Focus's Park Hill project is a 12-bed unit accommodating (for six to 12 months) refugees who have just left NASS support (details: HousingSupportTeam@focus.co.uk).

■ Access to housing through the 'homelessness' route

The 'homelessness' route is dealt with here because the reality is that new migrants often present as homeless and decisions will have to be made by local authorities. However, it is both government policy and good practice that authorities should prevent homelessness and develop alternatives that avoid this route being used, for a range of reasons including the welfare of people placed in temporary accommodation.

Access to housing through this route depends on the legislation and on the local authority's interpretation of it. This differs in England, Wales and Northern Ireland compared with Scotland.

Homelessness – England, Wales and Northern Ireland

In both England and Wales any applicant who is 'vulnerable' according to homelessness legislation is also considered to be in priority need. In England the code of guidance states that former asylum seekers:

> 'who have experienced persecution in their country of origin or severe hardship as a result of their efforts to reach the UK … may be vulnerable as a result'.

In Wales the guidance advises authorities that they *'should consider whether applicants who have suffered … harassment or violence on account of their gender, race, colour, ethnic or national origin, religion or sexual orientation'* are vulnerable. Both the English and the Welsh guidance also make specific reference to applicants with AIDs and HIV-related illnesses.

In England and Wales, as well as the ordinary priority need categories under homelessness legislation (old age, dependent children, etc) all 16 and 17 year olds are considered to be in priority need. In addition, in Wales all 18-20 year olds who were in care as a child or who are at risk of sexual or financial exploitation are in priority need. In England, 18-20 year olds are in priority need if they were in care while aged 16-18 (except certain full time students, who should be accommodated by social services).

In England and Wales, asylum seekers automatically establish a local connection in the last area in which they were accommodated by NASS (but not if they were in emergency accommodation or induction centres). This means that, assuming the applicant cannot establish a local connection by any other means (eg family ties), they can be referred back to the authority where their NASS accommodation was located. Special provisions apply where an applicant dispersed to Scotland applies in England or Wales, because the Scottish rules (see below) are different.

Homelessness in Northern Ireland is dealt with under part II of the Housing (Northern Ireland) Order 1988. It includes in the category of those who are considered to have priority need those who are vulnerable for a 'special reason'. There is however no code of guidance in Northern Ireland to give advice on how this should be interpreted.

Homelessness – Scotland

Under Scottish homelessness legislation, refugees may be considered vulnerable under various headings, depending on their needs. In particular, 18-20 year olds who have left local authority care, and people who by virtue of their ethnic or national origins are at risk of violence or harassment, are identified as priority needs categories. Unlike in England and Wales, refugees leaving NASS accommodation are not held to have a 'local connection' with the area providing the accommodation: refugees are free to present themselves as homeless to any authority.

In England, Wales and Scotland, local authorities which have not yet done so should review their policies and procedures to ensure that they cater both for the circumstances of refugees in housing need and for the short timescale in which they are likely to need accommodation. For example, it may be possible to accept single refugees as 'vulnerable' and in 'priority need' under homelessness legislation, based on evidence of post-traumatic stress or other conditions resulting from their experience as refugees. Prevention of homelessness among refugees should be part of a local authority's homelessness strategy.

■ Eligibility to register for social housing

Access to permanent social housing depends on legislation and on the local rules deciding who can apply through the housing register, waiting list or lettings schemes. Local authorites should be wary of indirectly discriminating against particular groups. Some councils (eg Leicester) have altered their policies to ensure that residence in NASS accommodation counts towards such requirements.

Choice-based lettings (CBL) schemes may also be an obstacle to refugees unfamiliar with how to apply or with poor English. RHA has started a choice-based lettings project intended to improve refugees' access to such schemes. The project will build the capacity of RCOs and RHA to develop and make use of community volunteers, who will assist refugees to make CBL bids using internet facilities. The project also aims to increase understanding of CBL, local services and refugee needs among all stakeholders (RHA contact details are in appendix 6).

■ Private sector housing

Many refugees and other new migrants, even if eligible for social housing, may opt for renting or lodging in the private sector and perhaps later to buy as owner-occupiers. Especially in areas where there is a shortage of accommodation, local authorities may want to facilitate both renting (see Oxford's Home Choice Scheme, page 44) and lodging (see the Praxis hosting scheme, page 42).

As mentioned above, a high proportion of asylum seekers and refugees are single people (often young men), and may have difficulty in accessing social housing, especially in areas of housing shortage. Private sector accommodation, often in hostels, multi-occupied properties or through sharing, is frequently the only available option. Clearly the quality of such accommodation and of its management, levels of rents and security of tenure are important issues – even more so for refugees and new migrants who may lack language and other skills necessary to relate to landlords or agents.

Overcrowding and sharing (even of bedrooms) often occur because people are under pressure to accommodate friends or relatives – particularly those who are destitute (see below). Health workers dealing with new migrants report this as a growing problem with both physical and mental health implications.

Difficulties in accessing private accommodation because of the need for rent deposits may be overcome by a rent guarantee or bond scheme. A guide to refugee-related schemes is published by hact (see appendix 6). The National Rent Deposit Forum (www.nrdf.org.uk) supports local deposit/bond schemes.

Services provided by environmental health and other enforcement staff are important ways of trying to minimise possible exploitation of vulnerable people and ensure that they have adequate standards of accommodation at reasonable rents. The Chartered Institute of Environmental Health publishes standards for asylum seeker accommodation in the private sector.

Accepted refugees who have been living in NASS-supported private accommodation (eg hostels) may well stay on in the same accommodation if the landlord also has units available for refugees. When refuges move into general private sector property such as houses in multiple occupation, the protection and services offered by regular inspections, and newly-developing licensing schemes, are very important. Section 2 of this chapter includes examples of private accommodation leased to refugee or other community-based organisations – this can be an effective way of using the private sector while also providing a management service sensitive to refugees' needs.

Floating support services (see chapter 5) are particularly useful for those living in the private sector who may not get the same housing management service that would be available through social housing. Similarly, housing advice centres or one-stop shops for asylum seekers and refugees (see chapter 5) can also provide assistance on private sector housing issues.

❑ Routes into accommodation and support – other new migrants

Some of what has been written about refugees also applies to other new migrants. There are limitations on the help which local housing authorities can give to some migrants from EU states (see appendix 3). Although working EU migrants generally are eligible for help under homelessness legislation and for allocation of local authority housing, many start in the private sector – with the same problems of insecurity and possibly poor conditions as apply to single refugees. In some cases, especially where the migrants are from the new EU countries, they may lose entitlement to benefits and housing if they lose their jobs and are unable to find alternative work, and so can become destitute.

In Northern Ireland, for example, many EU migrants are in jobs like farming and food processing. Examples of people losing jobs and having no entitlement to public help have led STEP (the South Tyrone Empowerment Programme – www.stepni.org) to work with new migrants with the aim of creating a hostel/support facility and also access to the housing market via a self-build renovation scheme: both projects are at the planning stage.

In Scotland, the regulations and code of guidance permit 'other new migrants' from EU countries, including the new accession states, to gain access to housing through both the local authority lettings and the homelessness routes (see appendix 3).

❑ Rough sleeping and destitution

Even in areas where good services are available it is perfectly possible that people will 'fall through the net' and end up as destitute and/or sleeping rough. The support services for identifying and helping people in the resident population with no proper accommodation will need to be alert to the possible needs of asylum seekers, refugees and other new migrants – and to the limitations on the help local authorities can provide for some of these groups (for example, rejected asylum seekers, those refused NASS accommodation, and certain migrants from EU accession states).

Possible reasons for destitution among asylum seekers include:

- having to leave NASS accommodation because their asylum claim has failed but the government will not forcibly return them to their country
- being rejected for 'hard case' support or refusing it because of the conditions (see chapter 3 – for example in cases where an asylum application is refused, but there is no safe route for the person to be sent home)
- wanting to proceed with a legal claim or appeal, but unable to access legal advice
- NASS support being withdrawn before a decision on the asylum claim has been received (eg because the asylum seeker moved to another area without permission)
- cases rejected on appeal where further legal action (eg a 'human rights' claim) is pending
- administrative errors (eg NASS believes an asylum case has come to an end but in fact the person has lodged an appeal).

A study of 38 destitute asylum seekers in Coventry found that three-quarters were at the end of the asylum process (ie their claims had been rejected) but in the remaining cases support had stopped for other reasons. In a study in Leicester of 168 destitute people, the proportions were similar. Of the Leicester cases, 68 had been destitute for more than six months, and 32 had 'slept rough' at some point.

Support services for asylum seekers and refugees – especially one-stop shops, or services run by RCOs – are also likely to be a first port of call for people who are destitute or sleeping rough. Many of those seeking help are likely to be ineligible for local authority housing, benefits or even emergency care provided by social services departments. In these cases, support from charities, faith groups or RCOs may be the only available option, apart from friends and family. Some non-statutory advice services – such as the Coventry Refugee Centre (see page 69) or the ASSIST project in Sheffield – offer positive help to people in these circumstances that are outside the statutory system. Some local Red Cross offices have destitution services aimed at asylum seekers (see www.redcross.org.uk). In some areas (eg Leicester) health services for asylum seekers will help those who are destitute, although there are limitations on help available through the NHS.

In practice most destitute people are dependent on family or friends who often are themselves dependent on NASS (or on benefits) and therefore have very limited incomes.

Section 2: Practical Examples

❏ Accommodation and support for asylum seekers

Some local authorities and housing associations are involved directly in providing temporary accommodation for asylum seekers through NASS contracts. This may involve both accommodation and support, or just support. By providing accommodation through a contract, a local authority or association can better ensure that effective arrangements are in place for the point of decision.

Swansea council has a NASS contract and also provides support services to the asylum seekers accommodated through the contract. Safe Haven Yorkshire, which is jointly owned by two regionally-based housing associations, does the same (more detail on Safe Haven in chapter 7). Some associations provide NASS with accommodation through sub-contracts (eg Cube HA in Glasgow and SHAC in Northern Ireland).

Practical example
A local authority NASS contract

The City and County of Swansea has a contract with NASS for the provision of accommodation and associated services such as area induction and orientation, signposting to other agencies and service providers, and ongoing support to asylum seeker families. Since starting in November 2002, it has built partnerships with other providers in Swansea, the voluntary sector, social services, education and health departments as well as community groups and RCOs. This has helped secure the right level of service and a multi-agency approach to any crisis intervention.

The support workers in the asylum seekers and refugee team (ASART) have built up extensive knowledge of NASS and IND procedures. This enables them to help families address many of their problems and to integrate successfully in Swansea. Since 2004, ASART has added a refugee resettlement service to its operations.

More details: 01792 483150

Practical example
HA provides accommodation for asylum seekers

In 2000, Cube HA in Glasgow had over 100 vacant flats in four high-rise blocks in Maryhill. The association entered into a contract with the Scottish Consortium of Asylum Seekers to lease 50 properties to them and there began a period of consultation with local residents. They had the chance to voice their fears and concerns about asylum seekers moving into the area and the association also addressed the myths that appeared in the press.

→

Once asylum seekers began arriving in the estate, reaction from existing tenants was limited. But the association argues that the mix of lifestyles has not brought the problems found in other parts of Glasgow.

Within six months of the scheme starting, 20 more flats were let to a private company for the same purposes. The income from the contract was partly reinvested in the estate – renewing windows and improving estate security – and this was popular with residents.

The association has received a number of applications for housing from those who have become accepted refugees, not only from those originally housed in Maryhill, but also refugees from other parts of the city.

More details: headoffice@cubehousing.co.uk

■ Information for asylum seekers near the point of decision

Some authorities have produced housing information leaflets, translated into various languages, which explain the options that will be available to accepted refugees, including ways in which the local authority or housing associations may help.

Practical example
Housing for refugees leaflet

Leicester's leaflet is aimed particularly at asylum seekers who have or are expecting their decision letter from the immigration service and their notice to quit from NASS accommodation. It explains (in various languages) the housing options available and where help can be obtained. All asylum seekers in NASS accommodation receive the leaflet.

More details from Leicester Housing Options Service: 0116 222 2699

❑ Initial accommodation and support for refugees

■ Advice for refugees at the point of decision

In some places there are advice services such as Leicester's RASAP project available to refugees at the point of decision, where they can get immediate help with housing and with obtaining benefits. Nottingham has a service aimed at non-priority need cases, such as single people.

Practical example
Advice at the point of decision (1)

Leicester's Refugee and Asylum Seekers' Advice Project is a partnership between the Home Office, the city council and local organisations, managed by Leicester Race Equality Council, and now funded by the European Refugee Fund (see chapter 8), for which it has been independently evaluated.

Since it started in 2001 it has worked with over 1200 refugees to claim benefits and provide practical help with obtaining accommodation, particularly for those at the point of decision on their asylum claim. In 2004 it obtained on average nearly £3,500 for each client in new benefits.

More details from RASAP: 0116 299 9807

Practical example
Advice at the point of decision (2)

Nottingham City Council's service helps non-priority need refugees to access permanent accommodation. An accommodation worker helps individual refugees to apply for council and HA accommodation, advising them on options and enquiring on progress with housing offices. This fulfils the statutory advice and assistance duties towards these applicants, but also offers a much-enhanced service compared to what would normally be available.

The service was able to follow a template already used successfully by the voluntary sector to help other vulnerable groups to access accommodation, and was an adaptation of existing services to the specific needs of refugees.

The project has been in operation since March 2004 and has assisted over 50 refugees. It received four out of five stars when evaluated by the Home Office's European Refugee Fund evaluation consultants in November 2004.

More details: 0115 915 1433

■ Encouraging refugees to stay in the same area

Projects such as Bonvenon (overleaf) and Gateshead's Move on Service (see chapter 6) exist to help and encourage refugees who want to stay in the area to which they were dispersed.

Practical example
Encouraging refugees to stay in the area

Banks of the Wear Community Projects undertook research into the move-on housing needs of refugees leaving NASS dispersal accommodation in the North East. This first ever study of its kind identified the fact that, given the right support, up to 80 per cent of asylum seekers dispersed to the region would like to stay. The research has now moved through a feasibility study stage and into project development.

The Bonvenon Project – set up with initial funding from hact – is now developing a network of practical initiatives to improve housing options for refugees and enable more of those that wish to remain in the North East after obtaining a positive decision on refugee status, to do so.

More details: www.bowcp.co.uk

■ Temporary accommodation

In addition to the standard temporary accommodation which is available to homeless people generally, there may be scope for promoting or developing solutions particularly appropriate for refugees. Options include:

- allowing accepted refugees (particularly families) to retain NASS accommodation for a certain period, to allow a move direct into permanent accommodation (see Swansea and Leicester examples)
- 'hosting schemes' where either long-term residents or households from established refugee communities in the area agree to take newly-accepted refugees as lodgers; such schemes may be very appropriate for 18-20 year olds leaving 'care' arranged by social services departments.

Practical example
Refugee resettlement service

Swansea has a contract with NASS, but the council's refugee resettlement service (RRS) serves all new refugees in Swansea. At the point of decision refugees are referred to RRS for a homelessness application to be made. This is done shortly before notice to quit is served on their NASS accommodation, and activated immediately afterwards. If suitable permanent accommodation becomes available before the end of the 28 day period, a permanent move takes place. If not, the refugee may be allowed to stay temporarily in their NASS accommodation (if the council's) or will be rehoused temporarily (if a private landlord). Single people who are not vulnerable are not covered by these arrangements, however.

More details: 01792 483150

Practical example
Prevention of homelessness pilot

Leicester has a contract with NASS, and refugees at the point of decision are able to continue to rent the same accommodation through RHA (the leaseholders) for up to 14 weeks while permanent accommodation is arranged by the council. This is a pilot project which requires flexibility in the NASS contract so that the individual property can be removed from it temporarily. The diagram shows how the pilot works. So far (June 2005), 12 refugees have been able to retain their NASS accommodation in this way, and have avoided being treated as homeless and placed in hostels or B&B. The scheme, which also runs in Derby, is a pilot intended to cover the first 20 families in NASS accommodation who ask for local authority help with rehousing. (NB There is currently concern about whether the new NASS contracts will allow this flexibility.)

More details: 0116 252 6802

Figure 4.3: Leicester's prevention of homelessness pilot scheme – Action at the point of decision to allow refugees to remain in their NASS accommodation

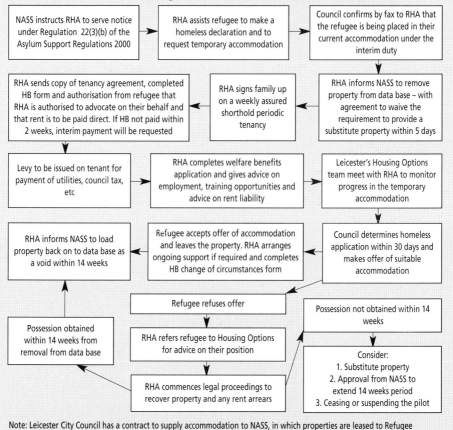

Note: Leicester City Council has a contract to supply accommodation to NASS, in which properties are leased to Refugee Housing Association (RHA) who administer the scheme and provide support to the occupants. RHA is part of the MHT group.

··

Practical example
Hosting scheme

Praxis is an independent charitable company working with asylum seekers and refugees. The hosting scheme is a community-based temporary accommodation service for London's refugees, placing young people (particularly) in local family homes. The aims are to offer a safe and welcoming space where newcomers can rebuild their lives and to promote positive community relations.

Demand has however been lower than expected: the scheme has placed around 35 people coming from five London boroughs. There is an independent evaluation of the scheme.

More details: www.praxis.org.uk/Hosting.aspx

··

❏ Permanent housing for refugees

■ Schemes solely for refugees

Some housing associations either set aside units to accommodate refugees, have a quota within their stock available for refugees or are willing to house refugees in standard properties and offer floating support services.

New Leaf (part of the Places for People group) has dedicated units in Sheffield for Somali and other refugees. Knightstone HA found that its Bristol stock was accommodating growing numbers of Somali people, and it responded by setting up a support service (see chapter 5).

··

Practical example
Specialist refugee housing project

New Leaf responded to a campaign by Somali people in Sheffield for more effective support for Somali refugees by using a block of six flats in a new development in Broomhall to provide both housing and a support service. The project later expanded to include larger family homes elsewhere.

The project now employs one Somali support worker, having widened its remit to cater for other refugee groups. It also provides ongoing support when residents move out of the scheme into general purpose accommodation. Currently the service is funded through Supporting People.

More details: www.placesforpeople.co.uk/newleaf/index.aspx

··

■ Accommodation for children and young people

Innovative accommodation solutions for young people include:

- hosting schemes such as Praxis (see above)
- foyers such as Portsmouth – combining accommodation with training opportunities. Other foyer proposals for young refugees are under development in Sheffield (Refugee HA) and Glasgow (Access Apna Ghar HA).

Practical example (in development)
Foyer to assist young asylum seekers

Access Apna Ghar, a non-registered BME housing association, is developing a foyer project to accommodate and offer training opportunities in the construction industry to 20 young refugees in Glasgow. Finance is from the Refugee Challenge Fund, and properties have been acquired on the open market using Housing Association Grant from the city council.

More details: apnaghar@cubehousing.co.uk

Self-build schemes involving refugees

Self-build or renovation schemes involving refugees are in their infancy but successful projects exist in Southwark and Leeds.

Practical example
Self-help renovation scheme using empty properties (1)

South Thames African Welfare Association (STAWA), an RCO, was helped by the Empty Homes Agency to develop an agreement with Southwark council to renovate and let empty properties. It lets these both to council nominees and to people on its own waiting list. It is also leasing private sector properties to expand its portfolio.

More details: 020 7703 5511

Practical example
Self-help renovation scheme using empty properties (2)

The Canopy Housing Project in Leeds is leasing and renovating empty properties owned by Leeds South Homes (one of the Leeds ALMOs). The aim is to provide accommodation, develop skills among the refugee population and other disadvantaged young people locally and promote good relationships within the Beeston Hill area. To date the project has renovated seven properties but is now expanding under hact's Accommodate programme.

More details: beecanhousing@ntlworld.com

■ Use of private sector accommodation

Many refugees will be housed in private rented accommodation. Two schemes illustrate ways of overcoming some of the problems they may face.

Practical example
Effective use of private sector accommodation (1)

Oxford had many asylum seekers who benefited from an amnesty for cases which were more than three years old and which received positive decisions. Liaison between housing staff, NASS and the social services department (responsible for pre-NASS cases) allowed longer-term accommodation to be provided in all cases. This was either by allowing the refugee to retain the short-term accommodation (leased from private landlords), or through the council's Home Choice Scheme, which provides tenancy deposits and rent in advance in the private sector, and also later checks with tenants and landlords at the time when the tenancy expires.

Home Choice has dealt with 108 former asylum seekers (June 2005), of whom 59 needed deposits or rent in advance at around £1,000 each. So far no families have become homeless, which would have been more disruptive as well as up to 40 times more expensive for the council to resolve. The housing department believes that this method has also given refugees a wider choice of where to live.

More details: homelessness@oxford.gov.uk

Practical example in development
Effective use of private sector accommodation (2)

The Midland Refugee Council (MRC) has developed a pool of managed properties in Birmingham and across the West Midlands for refugees who get leave to remain. To consolidate this service, MRC has recently formed a partnership with Birmingham Co-operative Housing Services (BCHS), a specialist HA which is part of Accord Housing Group, with considerable experience of providing management services to co-ops and community-based housing organisations.

MRC, with BCHS, now leases and manages almost 400 units owned by over 100 land-lords. BCHS manages the properties and MRC provides support services tailored to the needs of each household. The housing service is self-financing, primarily through HB payments, but it does require tight management and effective financial systems.

RCOs in the region have enquired about extending the service to cover properties that they are leasing. MRC are now looking to expand and develop their service while seeking wider partnerships with LAs and HAs for move on accommodation.

Most of the front-line work is undertaken by refugee housing workers either directly employed by MRC or seconded from MRC to BCHS. Various training programmes have been put in place to give them the opportunity to gain qualifications and pursue a housing career.

More details: from MRC on 0121 622 8858 or BCHS on 0121 764 3859

Checklist on accommodation issues

✓ is advice and information available on housing options for asylum seekers, refugees and new migrants in your area?

✓ have you considered the implications for your organisation of dealing with sensitive details, including their immigration status, about people who apply to you for help?

✓ if your organisation is a housing association, does its policies about lettings treat fairly people who are subject to immigration control, and not simply follow rules that only apply to local authorities?

✓ is there an effective arrangement for dealing with the housing needs of those leaving NASS accommodation?

✓ does this include the needs of young people, family reunion cases and disabled people?

✓ does your organisation's lettings policy – and those of other social housing agencies in your area – allow refugees access to housing, or does it discriminate against them directly or indirectly?

✓ when reviewing homelessness and allocations policies and practices in relation to race equality issues, have the needs of refugees been taken into account?

✓ can housing associations offer dedicated accommodation and support services for refugees in your area?

✓ do the support services for private tenants in your area take account of the special needs and difficulties encountered by asylum seekers and refugees?

✓ are there destitute asylum seekers in your area and are there (non-statutory) services which cater for them?

CHAPTER 5

BUILDING A NEW LIFE

What this chapter is about

- the practical support which people need
- options for providing support
- developing support services
- assessing what people need
- support needs in detail
- practical examples of support projects and services

If a home is important, how to pay for it, how to furnish and how to use it are equally so. Most new migrants need considerable initial support to make good use of their accommodation and to feel comfortable and secure in it. And as well as needs associated with the home, there are other immediate needs such as accessing health services and getting children into schools.

Many refugees and other new migrants also expect to live in the UK for a long period and naturally want to build a new life here, including learning English (for those who do not already speak it), being educated or trained, and finding a job. Many refugees have skills which they can use, if they can improve their English and receive further training.

This chapter concentrates on the needs of refugees and other new migrants whose status is decided and who are entitled to housing, welfare benefits and wider services. Much of it is relevant, however, to asylum seekers entitled to more limited help and who can generally only receive it through their NASS landlord or related support services.

Section 1: Policy and Good Practice Guidance

❑ Developing support services for individuals and families

Refugees and other new migrants are very diverse in their needs. Many are able to tackle the challenges of setting up a new life with just the help of some 'pointers'. At the other extreme, there will be individuals and families with a need for long-term intensive support. Ideally, organisations taking the lead in or co-ordinating support services should assess the range and levels of need within the new migrant population.

Although there are no hard and fast boundaries between support needs, chapter 3 divided them between housing-related needs (such as running the home, getting housing benefit), immediate wider needs (such as using local services like schools) and longer-term needs such as training and help with finding work. This division is also used in this chapter. Further community-related needs will be dealt with in chapter 6.

Many longer-term needs are unlikely to be met directly by housing professionals. They are included both to give a comprehensive picture and because housing organisations may be involved in identifying these wider needs through their support or resettlement services. Housing organisations may also help to establish services through multi-agency forums or through partnerships with other organisations, including ones with RCOs (see chapter 7).

■ Objectives of a support service

It is important for service providers to be clear about the objectives of a support service. RHA's general objectives for their East Midlands service are:

Refugee HA's floating support service – objectives

- provide a floating support service for refugees living in tenancies or newly allocated properties
- promote social inclusion to enable integration into British systems and institutions, sustain tenancies and integrate into the community
- provide support during and following a move to a new address
- provide tailored individual support, recognise their special needs as a vulnerable client group
- intervene in a proactive way in order to prevent and alleviate any crisis, promote independence

→

- ensure services are able to provide relevant support for tenants of all minority backgrounds
- ensure that external services the client is referred to have sufficient skills to provide practical support
- provide support for a period of up to two years depending on the needs of the individual.

This might translate into specific outcomes for individual clients such as:

- develop life skills to maintain independence
- make their house a home
- settle and integrate into the community
- understand and abide by the terms of the tenancy agreement
- be able to access a relevant range of statutory & voluntary sector services by themselves
- live comfortably with neighbours and the wider community to avoid the build up of problems.

The service will ideally provide a seamless transition from earlier support (eg in NASS accommodation) and also be flexible so as to 'float off' as the client becomes more independent. In Newcastle-upon-Tyne, for example, Stonham HA operates a floating support service covering both NASS cases and accepted refugees, tailored to individual needs; clients whose status changes experience no break in the service.

Compiling such a set of objectives, and relating these to the capacities of the organisation, will help to determine what services should be provided by the housing provider and which will require wider liaison to put them in place. Inevitably, there will be some 'fuzzy lines' between housing-related support and wider support. Those coordinating support services need to address questions such as:

- are the right levels of support available, covering all types of need?
- do projects duplicate each other, or leave gaps?
- what should general 'support packages' include to be most cost effective, and what is best handled by specialist services?

Chapter 9 (on strategy) makes the point that housing organisations should make themselves familiar with existing support services in their areas, what gaps there are and whether capacity exists to expand existing services rather than establish new ones. Especially for the wider support described later in this chapter, it may be better to negotiate access to or signpost existing services rather than start afresh.

■ Options for providing support

There is a range of options for providing support services:

- *Supported accommodation* where there are support workers on the premises or visiting on a daily basis.

- *Floating support* where the support worker visits and provides support in general needs social housing or private housing.

- *Advice or drop-in centres* which may be appropriate for single people, eg those living with friends.

- *Hosting or befriending schemes* where informal advice and practical help (eg with decorating or gardening) are provided by volunteers.

- *Specialist services* focussing on particular support needs such as health, training, or employment, or on particular groups such as women, disabled people, older people or refugees of particular nationalities.

Some support services are called 'resettlement' services; this chapter uses the term 'support' to include both.

It should be noted that support services aimed at specific groups (eg newly-arrived refugees from a particular country) are permitted under s35 of the Race Relations Act 1976, which allows 'positive action' of this kind provided there is objective evidence of the special need which is to be met.

The different options will need to be tested against the objectives set for the support service (see above). Ideally, either supported accommodation or floating support will be available (if needed) in all cases for those with stable housing arrangements, with advice centres as a 'back up' facility for other cases, and hosting or befriending as an 'add on' which enriches and extends the support arrangements and aids community integration. Government policy favours floating support as being more cost-effective than supported accommodation, while recognising that the latter might be necessary for some people who need high levels of support.

Funding for support services is dealt with in chapter 8, including the Sunrise programme and other initiatives under the government's strategy, *Integration Matters* (Home Office, 2005).

❏ Assessing support needs

■ Dealing with needs individually

While almost all refugees will require some support at the point of decision – particularly because few will have work, income or savings – their needs will differ, as will the time over which support will be needed. An individual assessment will enable the support to be tailored to the individual's or the family's needs, will enable agreement to be reached by 'both sides' on what is required, and will help ensure the most effective use of staff time. Such an assessment can help to identify the extent to which some of the support can be provided in other ways (eg by friends).

Ideally, the assessment will be carried out by the support worker, who will be experienced in identifying areas where support is likely to be needed, and what is already available. This also enables individual objectives to be set and progress reviewed as time elapses.

Chapter 4 referred to particular accommodation needs that might arise, such as housing and supporting children, reunited families and disabled people. Addressing such needs is obviously important too in providing support services. Some of these needs are referred to later in the chapter.

■ Developing a support plan

A personalised 'support plan' will not only identify the types of support required, but also act as a 'contract' between the support worker and the individual or family, in which both sides commit to certain tasks or targets.

Target times should be attached to the various support tasks, and kept under review. When it is agreed that support is no longer needed, it is also important to agree some regular review dates at which the support worker will revisit and check whether renewed support might be needed.

RHA uses a support plan produced jointly by the support worker and the client. In preparing and agreeing the plan, the worker goes through a number of standard items and discusses these individually with the client, and also takes account of other needs the client expresses.

A made-up example of such a plan is provided in figure 5.1 on the next four pages. The support needs given here are examples. An actual list may omit some of these and include others. The support worker should be able to deliver the basic 'package' of housing-related support, and make links with other workers or agencies for wider support services.

Where a service is to be funded through Supporting People there are further detailed requirements which are not dealt here but which apply to support services generally – further advice should be sought on these (see links at www.spkweb.org.uk).

The rest of this section looks at the support tasks in more detail.

Figure 5.1: Example support plan for refugee client

Refugee
Housing
Association

SUPPORT PLAN

Service user's name:	Mr S Plan
Address:	28 Support Street, Planning, Supporting. SP1 7SF
Support worker:	Ms Supporter (Ms S)
Needs (briefly list needs as identified at assessment eg welfare, health, etc)	Setting up home/welfare benefits/ health/ housing/ education
Date support plan to be completed:	20/01/06
How many goals are set out in this support plan?	5
Date support plan to be reviewed:	20/10/05
Support needs (high, medium, low) as identified at assessment	high/medium
No. of support hours per week:	1–2 hours

Figure 5.1: Example support plan for refugee client – contd.

SUPPORT PLAN GOALS/ACTIONS

Support need/area	*Setting up Home*
Support action/goal (What is the goal?)	*For Mr Plan to be able to furnish his flat and receive financial support from the social fund*

Target completion date: *30/08/05*	**Actual completion date:**

Proposed actions (What steps need to be taken in order to achieve the goal?)	**By whom** (who is responsible for each step?)	**By when**
Ms S to assist Mr Plan complete a community care grant form from the social fund.	*Ms S and Mr Plan*	*22/07/05*
Mr Plan to send the form by hand or post to the social fund.	*Mr Plan*	*22/07/05*
Ms S to assist with an appeal if need be.	*Ms S and Mr Plan*	*15/08/05*
If Community care grant awarded, Mr Plan to use this grant to buy furniture for his flat (Ms S may assist if need be).	*Mr Plan*	*25/08/05*

Support need/area	*Welfare Benefits*
Support action/goal	*For Mr Plan to be able to understand the welfare benefits system, ie apply for entitled benefits.*

Target completion date: *30/08/05*	**Actual completion date:**

Proposed actions	**By whom**	**By when**
Ms S to inform Mr Plan of what benefits he is entitled to and why.	*Ms S*	*25/07/05*
Ms S to assist Mr Plan complete relevant benefit forms which Mr Plan will then send.	*Ms S and Mr Plan*	*27/07/05*
Mr Plan to liaise with benefits agency thereafter (Ms S to assist if need be).	*Mr Plan*	*20/08/05*

Figure 5.1: Example support plan for refugee client – contd.

Support need/area	Health		
Support action/goal	For Mr Plan to register with a GP and local dentist		
Target completion date: 20/09/05		Actual completion date:	
Proposed actions		**By whom**	**By when**
Ms S to provide Mr Plan with all local GPs and dentists in his area.		Ms S	15/08/05
Mr Plan to visit or phone GPs and dentists to register (Ms S to assist if need be).		Mr Plan	30/08/05

Support need/area	Education		
Support action/goal	Mr Plan to enrol onto an ESOL class		
Target completion date: 30/12/05		Actual completion date:	
Proposed actions		**By whom**	**By when**
Ms S to inform Mr Plan of all enrolment dates at various colleges for an ESOL class.		Ms S	Ongoing until 30/12/05
Mr Plan to attend or phone college to arrange an interview for a possible enrolment date (Ms S to assist if need be).		Mr Plan	Ongoing until 30/12/05
Mr Plan to attend arranged ESOL classes.		Mr Plan	Jan 2006

Support need/area	Housing		
Support action/goal	For Mr Plan to liaise with the maintenance dept with regards to housing repairs.		
Target completion date: Ongoing		Actual completion date:	
Proposed actions		**By whom**	**By when**
Mr Plan to inform Ms S of all maintenance issues and repairs that require to be looked at.		Mr Plan	Ongoing
Ms S to assist Mr Plan contact maintenance dept and liaise with Housing Officer.		Mr Plan and Ms S	Ongoing
Mr Plan to be available at home for when maintenance dept visit his home.		Mr Plan	Ongoing

Figure 5.1: Example support plan for refugee client – contd.

YOUR SUPPORT PLAN IS NOW COMPLETED

Both you and your support worker can use the space below to make any final comments about your Support Plan and then sign. If there is any part of your assessment and support plan that you do not agree with then please comment below.

> *Ms S and Service user both happy with the support plan and agree to the proposed actions to be made.*
>
> *Service User does not require an interpreter for any of the above actions to be taken – understands basic English.*
>
> *Attending the ESOL class will improve Service User's knowledge, skills and abilities even further.*

Signed (Service user) _____ Signed (Support worker) _____

Signed (Team leader) _____ Dated _____

SUPPORT PLAN REVIEW

Present at review and their role:

Location: Date:

A number of support goals were agreed in your Support Plan. The purpose of the review meeting is to look at what progress has been made towards achieving each goal. It is important that a review is made of each goal individually with as much detail as possible. You may want to write about this yourself, or ask your support worker to write down what you say.

Support goal	Progress made

NEW GOALS

Recommendations (What new goals would you like your support worker to add to your Support Plan?)

Signed (Service user) _____ Signed (Support worker) _____

Signed (Team leader) _____ Dated _____

❑ Housing-related needs

■ Setting up and running the home

As emphasised before, newly-accepted refugees (in particular) are likely to be in a situation where they are about to lose (or have lost) their NASS-provided accommodation, normally equipped with furniture and other basics. Their income will have been at less than income support level, so most will start to set up their new home with next to nothing. And they may be moving to a new part of town with which they are unfamiliar.

Apart from the accommodation itself, their next most urgent need is likely to be furniture, basic kitchen appliances, etc. They can normally obtain these in two ways. The first is by obtaining a community care grant from the benefits office in order to buy them. (Leicester City Council has agreed with the local benefits office that they will 'fast track' applications so that the money is available within the 28-day period if possible.) The second method is through donations from charities which provide cash grants (eg for families with children) or services (eg recycling unwanted furniture). They may also need help with buying the goods or in moving whatever belongings they have from their previous accommodation.

Other immediate practical help is similar to that required for any new tenancy – decorating, connecting to utilities, learning how the heating works, arranging to install a washing machine, finding out how to report repairs, etc. Depending on their previous experience, refugees may be much less familiar with these practical aspects of everyday life and may need more help, quite possibly in their first language. People who are newly-arrived (eg asylum seekers) may need even more basic help with practicalities such as how domestic equipment works (the cooker, washing machine, etc). Bear in mind too that people may be unfamiliar with using the phone, that many services assume that phone contact can be made, and that this can be both inhibiting and expensive.

■ Paying for the home, applying for benefits and dealing with paperwork

Refugees are able to claim housing benefit and other benefits (income support, child tax credits, etc). They will need help not only in filling in forms but in pursuing claims. Where not combined with housing benefit, refugees may also need to claim council tax benefit from the local authority.

Some of the difficulties that can be encountered are shown by the following example from a refugee advice centre.

Example of benefit-related problems dealt with by an advice centre

Mr and Mrs X had made separate claims for asylum. They were still living in emergency accommodation when Mr X was granted indefinite leave to remain. His wife was now pregnant.

- The couple made a homelessness application and were deemed in priority need because of Mrs X's pregnancy. After several weeks in temporary accommodation they obtained a tenancy and were helped to claim a community care grant for furniture.

- There were difficulties obtaining HB because Mrs X's status meant she had no national insurance number (NINO), but it was eventually acknowledged that benefit can be paid without a NINO. (Refugees often encounter problems because the measures introduced to deter fraud amongst the settled community demand evidence that refugees cannot provide.)

- Mr X was entitled to backdated income support (now no longer available) because he was given refugee status but he never had 'proper' NASS support and was therefore unable to show the normal evidence (form NASS 35). Eventually evidence was obtained about the support Mr X had received and DWP made a backdated payment.

The couple were also helped to make successful claims for other benefits and Mr X was referred for help in finding suitable ESOL classes.

Although the advice centre was able to resolve this case, it illustrates the kinds of difficulty that might arise.

Dealing with correspondence, handling and budgeting for utility bills, getting a TV licence and using the postal service are also aspects of daily life where refugees may need more help than most tenants.

❏ Immediate wider needs

▓ Help with language problems

Even if a refugee is learning English, in the short-term there may be language problems in dealing with official forms and interviews. In some areas (eg Glasgow) there are general interpreting and translation services to overcome these difficulties and to help with a range of language needs. This is an aspect of support where partnership working can be particularly cost-effective – making sure that different services do not set up competing interpreter services, perhaps making use of the same limited resource of people with language skills. It is also an obvious area where refugees themselves may be recruited as workers or where RCOs can assist (see chapter 7).

■ Schools and services for children

Asylum seekers' children and those of other new migrants are both entitled and required to attend school, in the same way as any children living in the UK. Support services will often offer to help with initial contacts with schools. Praxis, the hosting scheme for young asylum seekers and refugees described in chapter 4, includes education as part of its service. In Glasgow, with its large numbers of asylum seekers/refugees, some schools have bi-lingual units to help children to integrate into mainstream education. In Bury, the asylum seekers team liaises with dedicated staff in the education department including a 'link worker' who supports families in establishing their children in school and deals with any difficulties arising.

Although wider practice by schools in dealing with new migrants, language requirements and multi-cultural issues in education is very important in assisting integration, it is outside the scope of this guide. The Qualifications and Curriculum Authority publishes guidance on meeting the needs of children newly-arrived from overseas (www.qca.org.uk/8476.html) and there is an email support group for teachers and others working with migrant children (www.refed.org.uk/).

Programmes such as Sure Start provide wider support for families with young children. As well as helping with school and health issues, they can help families build wider networks and assist integration (see example on page 83).

■ Access to health care

For asylum seekers, refugees and other new migrants securing access to health care is a further priority, and one on which there is no restriction relating to the migrant's status (except in the case of people refused asylum and who have exhausted the appeal process – see guidance on entitlement from the Department of Health – www.dh.gov.uk).

However, there are a number of potential obstacles:

- lack of familiarity with the NHS (people may have low expectations or – in contrast – be 'over-medicalised')
- cultural barriers to using the services or around certain issues (eg HIV/Aids)
- insufficient mental health services and over-stretched GP services in some areas
- inadequate interpreter services, in particular in the area of mental health
- lack of continuity of care especially as people move between accommodation
- forms, such as those giving exemption from charges, only being available in English and Welsh.

The British Medical Association believes that:

'… not enough is being done to safeguard asylum seekers' health. Basic medical testing does not routinely take place which means that tuberculosis often goes undiagnosed, those suffering from psychological affects of torture are not always referred to specialist centres, and unaccompanied children are not given appropriate vaccinations and immunisations'. BMA (2004) *Asylum Seekers and their Health.*

The BMA recommends that the physical and mental health of all asylum seekers (including children) should be assessed and appropriate treatment and/or support given. Medical assessment should include testing for TB, Hepatitis A, B, C and HIV (with appropriate counselling, and testing should not be mandatory), immunisation and vaccination. It should include assessment and referral to a specialist centre if there is any evidence of physical or psychological torture or maltreatment.

Many of the specialist refugee health projects that have been established act as a bridge between refugee communities and health services, offering help such as:

- identifying refugee health needs, especially needs that may be hidden, such as those of single women with children or people with mental health problems
- advice and promotional work on health issues (eg HIV/Aids)
- advocacy work with health services on behalf of refugees
- interpreting, often using refugees with both language and health care skills
- befriending, self-help schemes, drop-in centres and support groups
- counselling
- training for other professionals in recognising refugee health needs (especially mental health).

Torture and rape victims are likely to require specialist help, perhaps for many years. The Medical Foundation for the Care of Victims of Torture has (with REDRESS) published a guidance handbook (available at www.redress.org/publications/Handbook_En.pdf). It describes symptoms associated with torture, the possibility of treatment and of redress, and places where treatment is available across the UK.

Mental health problems such as post-traumatic stress may occur for various reasons, for example as a result of bad experiences (racist abuse, etc) in the UK. They may be exacerbated by overcrowding or sharing of accommodation.

'Housing is the key to stabilising a person's mental health. They have lost their house, their farm, their city, their job, their country. We have to start to reverse this process.'
Saeed Abdi, MAAN Somali Mental Health Project, Sheffield

Some asylum/refugee support services cover health issues. For example, the Bury asylum seekers team works jointly with the Primary Care Trust (PCT) to arrange health screening sessions at the local walk-in centre for newly arrived asylum seekers, and also has a system to ensure that all new arrivals are able to register with a GP. Bolton Community Homes is considering developing a specific support service for asylum seekers and refugees with HIV/Aids. It has also has plans to pilot a drug interventions community engagement project (see www.drugs.gov.uk). Sheffield Asylum Health Team works directly with accommodation providers and stresses the importance of these links (see page 66).

Finally, the Health for Asylum Seekers and Refugees Portal (www.harpweb.org.uk) provides a range of general health information.

■ Meeting disabled people's needs

In chapter 4, some of the difficulties encountered by disabled or chronically ill people were discussed. In relation to wider support, the National Information Forum publishes a comprehensive guide, *How to Access Disability Services*, aimed at those working with asylum seekers and refugees (see http://nif.org.uk/publications.htm).

A particular issue may be that of 'young carers' – people under 18 caring for adult disabled people or others with care needs. The Children's Society has a Young Carers Initiative which covers asylum/refugee cases (www.childrenssociety.org.uk/youngcarers).

■ Legal and immigration advice

Legal advice is important to asylum seekers up to the point of decision, and of course after it if the decision is negative:

- they may need help in pursuing their claims
- they may need help in securing support from NASS in cases where it has been refused
- asylum seekers whose applications are rejected may need help to appeal and/or take action under human rights legislation;

and refugees may need advice about:

- bringing family members to the UK
- citizenship
- challenging the decision on their status (if they were not given indefinite leave to remain).

Some of the issues about availability of legal and immigration advice are:

- possible problems of access for asylum seekers dispersed to areas with limited advice services, or where it is difficult to coordinate legal advice with necessary interpreter services

- restrictions on legal aid, placing increasing limits on the free advice available
- complaints about the quality of legal advice services
- legal restrictions on non-qualified people giving immigration advice, so that general advice workers have to be careful about the kind of help they give (this does not apply to advice about getting NASS support).

Advice is available from a range of sources, such as:

- solicitors and barristers specialising in immigration (some of whom are funded by the government's Legal Services Commission – LSC)
- specialist non-profit advisers, funded by the LSC, who must be approved by the Office of the Immigration Services Commissioner (OISC)
- national advisory services such as the Refugee Legal Centre (www.refuge-legal-centre.org.uk) and the Immigration Advisory Service (www.iasuk.org)
- non-specialist community/voluntary sector advisers, normally providing advice on asylum/refugee issues generally (must also be approved by OISC)
- commercial immigration advisers or consultants, who must be approved by OISC.

In Northern Ireland, the Law Centre provides immigration advice and they report that the availability in the province of lawyers experienced in this field is very limited indeed.

Although unlikely to be able to offer legal advice themselves, housing organisations providing support services will want to ensure that there are good links with services that do offer such advice. Ideally, there will be proper referral arrangements, including a system for notifying who has capacity to take on cases (like that operated by the Yorkshire and Humberside Consortium), and arranging interpreting when needed (which legal aid may pay for).

❑ Longer-term needs

■ Learning English

> *'It has been a culture shock coming here by myself but I'm now working hard to improve my English so that I can get a job'*
> Kurdish refugee, The Guardian (2001) *Welcome to Britain.*

Many asylum seekers and refugees do have some English language skills, but often insufficient to take full advantage of training or work opportunities. Only 17 per cent of new arrivals speak English well.

Initially, the emphasis of support may be on interpretation, but this is likely to move quickly on to improving the English of the new migrants themselves. English language training is one of the support services that can be accessed by asylum seekers before their point of decision. Of course, adequate English language skill becomes even more important for the accepted refugee or long-term migrant.

Support or resettlement services normally have contacts with local ESOL courses, which may be free or have favourable fees for new migrants. (Bury asylum seekers team has worked with local colleges to ensure adequate ESOL provision for approximately 430 asylum seekers and refugees living in the district.) However, Home Office research shows that there is a shortage of classes and long waiting lists for ESOL courses in many areas.

Work-related training and job opportunities

Research by the National Institute for Adult Continuing Education (NIACE) has shown that those who have been granted permission to remain in the UK and those who have been given permission to work while their applications are being considered face various barriers to finding employment:

- not having any UK work experience or knowledge of the systems
- not having any UK references
- overseas qualifications not recognised
- not having opportunities to prove skills or develop them further
- potential employers having negative attitudes to employing refugees
- psychological problems for asylum seekers resulting from, among other things, lack of purposeful activity during the 'waiting period' and consequent low self esteem.

Centrepoint (2004) has reached similar conclusions about the work-related barriers met by young refugees. Women refugees may be deterred from joining mixed training groups and generally face greater obstacles than men in getting jobs.

Support or training services to help overcome these barriers are therefore very important. Home Office-sponsored research also argues that such services are more effective 'when in close proximity to initiatives looking after housing, welfare and other practical needs' (Carey-Wood, J, 1997).

These examples illustrate the variety of approaches that exist to helping refugees into work (and more detailed examples follow in section 2):

- Brent's Refugees into Jobs project, established with SRB funding (see Housing Today, 24 September 2004).
- Accord HA in Walsall has used a local 'Steps to Work' scheme (www.stepstowork.walsall.org.uk) to give work experience to refugees, possibly leading to full-time appointments.

- Foyers, which combine accommodation for young people with training/employment opportunities, can assist young refugees (see www.foyer.net and chapter 4).
- Glasgow's Wise Group has a programme called ASSIGN, aimed at asylum seekers (www.thewisegroup.co.uk/assign/index.html).
- the Refugee Women's Empowerment Project is aimed at capacity building for women refugees, better equiping them for work (www.refugeewomen.org/rwa.htm).
- Refugee Education and Training Advisory Service (RETAS) helps refugees (especially women) get their qualifications recognised (www.education-action.org).

Many of the practical examples in this chapter, and elsewhere in the guide, have recruited refugees as staff members, for their language and other skills. Rainer, a national charity working with under-supported young people including refugees, has in its Lincoln project employed several Iraqi Kurd refugees as support workers, who also raise awareness in the community about refugee issues (www.raineronline.org).

Specific resources exist to encourage refugees from certain professions into new employment. For example, there are an estimated 1,000 refugee doctors who could work in the NHS, and the Rose website (www.rose.nhs.uk) has material to assist these and other health professionals back into work. The TUC and CARA (Council for Assisting Refugee Academics) offer a handbook to help academics convert their skills after being granted leave to remain (e-mail: info@cara.lsbu.ac.uk).

It is beyond the scope of the guide to go into more detail on employment issues, but the DWP now has a refugee employment strategy, *Working to Rebuild Lives*, which contains a range of proposals and information on current initiatives (www.dwp.gov.uk/publications).

■

Section 2: Practical Examples

❏ Options for housing-related and wider support services

The chart opposite [check] sets out basic information on five asylum/refugee support services in different parts of the country. The chart is intended to facilitate comparisons between the characteristics of the different services – funding, staffing and the scope of the services provided.

Other projects mentioned in this guide are also relevant to the practical support needs of refugees and other new migrants – for example, the Bonvenon project (see page 40) and the support provided by the Upper Pennywell Residents' Association, also in Sunderland (see page 82).

Figure 5.2: Support services – five examples

Project	Funding	Staffing	Starts at asylum stage?	Dedicated accommodation?	Furniture etc	Advice about the house itself	Benefits advice	Utility bills	Budgeting	Correspondence	Help with obtaining TV licence	Help with postal service	Help with language problems	School liaison	Health care liaison	Legal/immigration advice	ESOL liaison	Help with training/work	Other
Leicester – RHA floating support scheme	Supporting People	Team leader and five floating support officers plus other supporting staff	(1)		●	●	●	●	●	●	●	●	●	●	●	(2)	●	●	Floating support service for up to two years based on 'support plan' agreed between client and worker
Liverpool – CDS floating support service for people with leave to remain	CDS with Housing Corporation I&GP Grant and Supporting People	Senior floating support officer and two basic grade officers			●		●	●	●	●	●	●	●	●	●	(3)			Floating support for up to two years, depending on 'support plan' agreed between client and worker
Gateshead MBC – Move on Service	Supporting People	Three refugee support workers plus admin worker	(1)		●	●	●	●	●	●	●	●	●	●	●	(3)	●		Floating support for up to about a year, with reviews thereafter; prioritises vulnerable people
Bradford Community Housing Trust – asylum team	Part of NASS contract	Manager, seven support workers and other staff inc. maintenance and cleaning	●	●	●	●	(4)	●			●		●	●	●		●	n/a	Basic service aimed at asylum seekers in temporary accommodation
Bournemouth Churches HA – Refugee Support Team	Supporting People	Two floating support workers report to a team leader (who has a wider brief)				●	●	●		●	●	●	●	●	●	(3)	●	●	Service supports a caseload of 36 refugees and their families; aimed especially at wider support needs

Notes: (1) ties in with separate asylum support service (2) assistance with family reunion issues (3) signposting to a specialist service (4) in cases where there is a positive decision

One of the services in the chart has been independently evaluated:

Practical example
A floating support service that has been independently evaluated

Cooperative Development Services (CDS) piloted a floating support service using Housing Corporation I&GP grant, which was then evaluated (see web link below) to provide good practice lessons. The service provided housing and a range of practical support measures, including furniture packs. As a service innovation, tools such as needs assessment methods and support plans were devised from scratch. The independent evaluation concluded that the pilot was successful. Good practice lessons included:

- CDS has a strong base in offering support services generally and this helped considerably in setting up the new service
- the pilot was treated as a learning experience and the team was able to adapt it as they went along; CDS supported them in this
- the support task is demanding and workers need good resources and 'back up' to tackle problems that emerge
- the pilot was clear about its expected outcomes, it delivered them and was able to show evidence of delivery
- networks (or partnerships) had a vital role to play and CDS were committed to developing them.

The support service secured Supporting People funding on a long-term basis.

More details: www.cdshousing.org.uk/news.asp?type=4

Unlike these general support services, the Latin American Women's Rights Service caters only for older women:

Practical example
A support service for older women

The Islington-based Latin American Women's Rights Service (an RCO) operates an advice and support service for older women, focusing on housing, welfare rights, personal finance and issues such as abuse and domestic violence. Many of the problems it encounters are the result of poor housing conditions, or poor relationships with younger family members, and it has developed referral arrangements with two housing associations. The project is financed by hact's older people's programme and has been recently evaluated.

More details: www.womeninlondon.org.uk/lawrs.htm

An interesting response to emerging support needs from a refugee community was made by Knightstone HA:

Practical example
A support service for Somali tenants

Knightstone found that in its Bristol properties it had a growing proportion of Somali tenants with English language difficulties, and responded by creating a Supporting People-funded support service on housing-related matters which tenants can receive for up to two years. Staff with Somali language skills are available and basic tenancy correspondence is translated. The aim is to enable clients to develop the skills needed to manage their tenancies themselves, and also link them in with other sources of support within the community.

More details: 01934 524300

❏ Practical examples of support on particular issues

■ Help with language problems

A particularly innovative approach has been shown by Newlon HA's partnership with other housing providers in their area of London.

Practical example
Interpreter/translation service based on local language skils

In partnership with five other associations, Newlon helped establish the ARTICLE service to provide quality interpreter and translation services. They assessed their needs and their existing costs, and decided that it would be cost effective to set up a dedicated service based on the skills of their tenants. This required potential interpreters to complete a training course. ARTICLE is now a co-op, with a part-time co-ordinator, offering services to the housing sector throughout this part of London, outside normal hours if required.

The ARTICLE service has won awards, including a National Housing Award in 2004, and Newlon have published a guide to help other organisations set up similar services. An evaluation of the service is also planned in 2005.

More details: info@articletranslation.co.uk or regeneration@newlon.org.uk

■ Access to health care

Three services are highlighted here. The first two address the difficulties mentioned earlier about asylum seeker/refugee access to health care; the third is a response to mental health care needs in a particular refugee community.

Practical example
A dedicated health team (1)

Sheffield has an asylum health team which responds to the difficulty of providing asylum seekers with access to GP services. The services they provide include:

- working with accommodation providers to register all new arrivals and provide a direct GP service
- screening for a range of illnesses
- guidance on how to get the best out of the NHS
- bringing people up-to-date with immunisations and standard tests
- treatment for the full range of conditions
- experienced use of interpreter services
- registration with a regular GP after the point of decision

The team has developed specialist knowledge about refugee health needs and cultural issues about health care. It consists of four nurses, a dedicated GP, a half-time counsellor and four bi-lingual support workers (including refugees). A physiotherapist provides one session per week. Funding is mainstream NHS.

More details: Joan.Macfarlane@sheffieldse-pct.nhs.uk

Practical example
A dedicated health team (2)

In Hillingdon, the initiative to provide more effective health services for asylum seekers and refugees was taken by the PCT itself. The 'Hope Project', which has succeeded in registering more than 500 people who previously were not registered with a GP, is a partnership with local voluntary groups. It has:

- primary health care workers who carry out outreach health sessions and health assessments and an advice worker for asylum seekers and refugees
- developed a network of interpreters and advocates from within the refugee/asylum communities
- funded the production of a directory of services for asylum seekers and refugees in Hillingdon
- run a woman's group for asylum-seeking woman who have post-natal depression
- developed language-based woman's groups
- funded training for asylum seekers and refugees in health advocacy and interpreting
- provided targeted health promotion sessions.

HOPE won a Guardian Public Services Award for services to asylum seekers in 2004.

More details: www.hillingdon.nhs.uk

Practical example
A refugee mental health project

Set up by refugees in response to the needs of Sheffield's 6,000 Somali residents, the MAAN project acts as a two-way link between people with mental health problems and the health service. It employs seven staff, including a Somali psychiatrist. It has both a supported housing project and a floating support service. It has developed specialist interpreting expertise and also understanding of the cultural differences in dealing with mental health problems – for example the stigma associated with mental illness and therefore the difficulty of using volunteer workers because people are reluctant to discuss problems with them.

More details: *Volume*, issue 7, summer 2004 (see www.hact.org.uk)

■ Learning English

In Glasgow, the city's 'integration networks' have provided less formal language training to complement college-based courses.

Practical example
Language training through local networks

Glasgow has ten such networks established between 2000 and 2002 in different parts of the city. Some offer informal conversational English classes, often with crèche facilities, and sometimes run by volunteers. The informal classes are popular with women, although because they do not offer formal qualifications this may put the women at a disadvantage. This has led to the identification of the need for women-related facilities at colleges, and has also led to the integration of language training with other courses, for example a 'women and business' course provided by one network.

More details: Wren, K (2004)

In Leicester, in addition to ESOL facilities, there is a complementary course for organisations in the city dealing with people whose second language is English.

Practical example
ESOL awareness-raising training

Leicester Adult Education College provides awareness training for organisations which have regular contact with people whose first language is not English. The training package covers:
* cross-cultural differences
* listening and pronunciation difficulties of ESOL speakers
* literacy issues
* contacts with other organisations.

More details: 0116 233 4343

■ Work-related training and job opportunities

In the East Midlands, contact between senior housing officials and NIACE led to the establishment of the Asset UK project in the region.

Practical example
Survey of needs leads to specialist service being established (1)

In January 2001, NIACE was funded by the East Midlands Development Agency to undertake a skills and qualifications audit of asylum seekers in Leicester, to discover what skills and qualifications they had and the potential contribution that they might make to the local economy.

The research revealed that a high percentage of those surveyed possessed qualifications ranging from school leaving certificates to higher degrees, including vocational and professional qualifications, and had been in paid skilled employment before they came to the UK. The majority spoke more than one language and many had engaged in voluntary work and secondary occupations.

The research also highlighted considerable barriers to fulfilling their aspirations. NIACE secured funding from the European social fund EQUAL initiative in 2001 to employ five project workers to audit the skills, qualifications and experiences of asylum seekers across the East Midlands and to create tailored opportunities for volunteering and labour market orientation alongside learning support. By 2004, 259 placements had been made.

More details: www.niace.org.uk/projects

In Tyne and Wear, BoW Community Projects conducted a survey of skills and learning needs among asylum seekers and refugees so that provision could be improved. Although not strictly related to housing needs, it is part of BoW's general work in helping to ensure that asylum seekers stay in the North East at the point of decision and that facilities are attractive to them.

Practical example
Survey of needs leads to specialist service being established (2)

This survey for the Learning and Skills Council identified the wide range of skills possessed by asylum seekers and refugees, and their aspirations to learn English and develop other skills. It also found that, while aspirations to train and find jobs are one of the most important factors in accepted refugees staying in the region, only a small proportion of them had received advice on these issues. The report has helped to inform the development of ESOL and job-related training courses in the region. BoW carried out the study in partnership with RETAG Support Services – a refugee-led employment initiative.

→

BoW is now working with the Regional Refugee Forum NE and other partners including the Regional Development Agency on the Inroads Project – an initiative to improve enterprise opportunities for refugees and other new in-migrants to the North East.

Summary of report: www.bowcp.co.uk/LSC%20Report.pdf

Many support services offer training and employment advice as a part of their service. Coventry Refugee Centre has a dedicated service funded by the Learning and Skills Council.

Practical example
Job-related advice in a refugee centre

The Coventry advice service offers the following:
- impartial and objective advice and guidance to refugees and asylum seekers on ways into employment
- after an in-depth interview, clients are referred to employers/other agencies/organisations – they can then return for further aid and advice as many times as they wish
- guiding each client through a step-by-step process to achieve employment until such a time when the client starts to work
- presenting options in a way which helps the client's understanding of the UK job market and enables him/her to make informed decisions.

Support and encouragement is offered to encourage the client to follow paths that will open his/her horizons and lead towards sustainable work.

More details: www.coventry-refugee-centre.org

Some organisations have enlisted volunteers from among local residents to help with informal training – thus also assisting community relations and understanding. Charter's scheme was judged as the 'outstanding achievement in the UK' in the 2005 National Housing Awards.

Practical example
A skill-sharing scheme

Learning Links, operating largely in the Pill area of Newport, brings together older residents with practical or language skills, and young people (such as asylum seekers) and other vulnerable groups. For example, an older resident who speaks Arabic and is keen on bike maintenance has been sharing his skills with young Iraqi asylum seekers. Other 'shared skills' have included passing the written part of driving tests, cooking, family budgeting and homemaking.

Learning Links is part of the EQUAL programme, funded by the European social fund.

More details: www.charterhousing.co.uk and in Inside Housing, 12 November 2000

A final example from Sheffield offers work-shadowing placements to refugees from professional backgrounds.

Practical example
Work shadowing for refugees with professional backgrounds

The Refugee New Arrivals Project originated in May 2001. Recently it has embarked upon some new activities including organising work shadowing for skilled refugees with a good level of English. Through partnerships with employers, it offers refugees a chance to observe the work of similar professionals in Britain, understand the work culture, and identify training they need to be able to re-enter their professional field. The project believes it also helps employers by improving the image of their organisation, helping to develop coaching skills and enhance multi-cultural understanding among their staff, and possibly encouraging skilled people to apply for jobs with them in the future.

The project has set up professional support groups (one for teachers that has developed into a structured course, and one for engineers at the planning stage).

It has been funded through the Home Office Challenge Fund, Tudor Trust and the Big Lottery Fund.

More details: 0114 241 2785

Checklist on support issues

✓ Is there any assessment of the support needs of new migrants in your area?

✓ Does anyone know what range of services exists, and where the gaps are?

✓ Do mainstream providers like the health service understand the needs of new migrants, and adapt their services accordingly?

✓ Does the Supporting People programme reflect new migrants' needs?

✓ Can lessons be learnt from other support services, in developing new ones for asylum seekers, refugees and other new migrants?

CHAPTER 6

LIVING IN A COMMUNITY

What this chapter is about

- aims for work at the community level
- improving personal understanding between people
- providing information and 'myth busting'
- ways of bringing people together
- creating local networks
- helping people feel secure
- changing perceptions more widely
- practical examples of community-level initiatives

In looking at the place of new migrants in the wider community, there is a need to consider the issues from the viewpoints of both the new migrants themselves *and* those of the communities where they are going to live or are already living. The studies that have been carried out which have looked at relationships at community level (for example, D'Onofrio and Munk, 2004) have emphasised the similarity of what people commonly want – such as a feeling of safety, being accepted, having the opportunity to make friends, etc. A common language and some knowledge of each other's culture are also important in the two-way process of people getting to know each other.

The issues are similar whether considered at the level of the individual person or family, at the level of a neighbourhood or estate, or across a whole city. What practical steps can housing organisations and others take, both to promote positive relations between people and to tackle negative reactions such as racist harassment?

At national level, there are government policies on both 'refugee integration' and 'community cohesion', as well as statutory duties to promote good race relations. The chapter considers briefly how local action fits within the national policy framework. Some local authorities have a 'refugee integration strategy' or a 'community cohesion strategy' and their role is considered further in chapter 9 which looks at strategic issues.

This chapter looks first at different ideas about what organisations should aim to achieve at community level. Then it considers the kinds of activity needed – improving personal understanding, providing information, bringing people together, creating networks, helping people feel secure and changing perceptions more widely. Finally, it includes practical examples to illustrate different approaches.

Section 1: Policy and Good Practice Guidance

❑ Aims at community level

Defining objectives for wider work in the community is much more difficult than for providing accommodation and supporting individuals, because of the need to take account of the opinions both of new migrants and of established communities, and the fact that views are likely to differ from one person to another. A Home Office study (Ager and Strang, 2004) of refugee and non-refugee residents of two very different areas, one in Glasgow and one in London, nevertheless found many common threads. Some people simply expect there to be 'no trouble' in the community, others expect some 'mixing' to take place (being accepted and people being friendly), and others actively want a sense of 'belonging' (having friends from different groups in the area, and shared values such as treating older people respectfully).

The headings in this chapter reflect the range of issues that people might want to tackle at community level. A useful exercise, before starting any community-level work, is to consider which of these issues are important locally. This could be done by:

- 'brainstorming' among the staff team working in the area
- listening to the experience of other community-level workers (teachers, police, etc)
- talking to residents' group leaders and other community representatives (eg in places of worship or local advice centres)
- consulting refugee community organisations – either those in the neighbourhood (where they exist) or city-wide groups
- reviewing some of the published material referred to in this chapter (see appendix 7 for details) and elsewhere.

Ideally, this kind of planning should take place well before new migrants start to move into an area – but if it takes place later then local views (and prejudices that may have developed) must of course be taken into account.

Both practitioners and people in the community (whether long-term residents or newcomers) can benefit from looking at what has been done elsewhere (eg finding out about or even jointly visiting some of the projects mentioned in section 2).

Setting the aims of a project is a task best done at local level, informed by local views about the expectations and priorities that people have. Ideally, there will be a 'support plan' a little like the one considered in chapter 5, but for the community not the individual. This chapter should help to establish what a local 'community support plan' might include.

■ What does the government expect?

But there are also UK government policies about 'integration' and 'community cohesion' which programmes and projects at local level will need to take into account – especially if they hope to gain official funding or (in the case of housing organisations) are regulated by government agencies.

The Home Office's (2005) strategy defines integration as:

> *'the process that takes place when refugees are empowered to achieve their full potential as members of British society, to contribute to the community, and to become fully able to exercise the rights and responsibilities that they share with other residents.'*

Officially, integration is what happens (or should happen) to an *individual*. There is a separate definition (LGA and others, 2002) of what should happen at *community* level, where the aim is 'community cohesion'. A cohesive community is defined as one where:

- *'there is a common vision and a sense of belonging for all communities;*
- *the diversity of people's different backgrounds and circumstances are appreciated and positively valued;*
- *those from different backgrounds have similar life opportunities; and*
- *strong and positive relationships are being developed between people from different backgrounds in the workplace, in schools and within neighbourhoods.'*

The idea of promoting community cohesion came not from work with new migrants but from conflicts between different ethnic groups in three northern cities in 2001. However, it has become increasingly relevant to new migrant communities, particularly since the issues of 'asylum seekers' and 'immigration' have become confused and overlap with each other in political debate and in the media. Folow up guidance (LGA and others, 2004) emphasises the importance of taking account of asylum seekers and refugees, and gives practical examples. There are also separate CIH guidance and case studies on community cohesion generally.

In addition to government policy, public bodies have a statutory duty to promote good race relations and this translates (for example) into the Housing Corporation's regulatory requirement to 'promote good relations between people of different racial groups'. Action of the kind discussed in this chapter will therefore help organisations demonstrate that they are fulfilling these duties.

❑ Elements of a 'community support plan'

■ Improving personal understanding between people

At the most basic level, an individual can only start to feel part of a community if he/she can communicate with other people, especially people who are not part of their own group. So what was said earlier about learning English (where a new migrant does not have good English already) is essential so that people have a common language through which to understand each other.

A further need though is what can be called 'cultural understanding'. This can range from day-to-day issues like attitudes to litter or attitudes to older people, between different communities, to bigger ones like respecting religious differences and one community starting to understand the culture of another. The Glasgow/London study (Ager and Strang, 2004) showed that people are willing to accept different cultural practices in an area if they can find a way of discussing and resolving any difficulties.

Some points about this – from *Understanding the Stranger* (D'Onofrio and Munk, 2004) – are:

- don't assume any knowledge on the part of the host community – they will have questions and need information on some quite basic issues (see below)
- many asylum seekers, in particular, are very preoccupied with their asylum cases and may feel that they have been accommodated only temporarily in a particular place – so may take a while to engage with the host community
- many asylum seekers are young men, have very limited resources and are generally not allowed to work – so it is not surprising that they spend time hanging around in public places with their friends.

What might be called 'closing the gap' between cultures is of course likely to be easier if the area is already multi-cultural and new migrants do not stand out so readily. However, experiences in places like Glasgow show that although asylum seekers moving into a predominantly 'white' area can be very difficult, it can also (perhaps after initial problems) be made to work. Refugees interviewed in the Glasgow/London study found they were accepted in some cases by older Glasgow residents who welcomed the fact that people were moving into an apparently declining estate. Cube HA in Glasgow recycled money it received from its NASS accommodation into estate improvements, and told residents it was doing so, helping to promote good relations (see page 37).

In areas where new migrants are already living, it is important to find out if relations with long-term residents reveal any issues that should be addressed. As mentioned above, contact with front-line workers, tenants' and residents' groups or new migrants' representatives can all be useful in building up a picture of local relations. This should include asking about the position of particular groups – such as young people or women – and whether all ethnic groups are in contact with each other or some are marginalised. It cannot be assumed that people from the same ethnic group, or the same religion, necessarily 'get on'.

Particular problems have been reported in various places recently because of the growing numbers of destitute asylum seekers (see chapter 4). If people have no formal income or means of support, they may be heavily reliant on other members of the same community, possibly resulting in tension and overcrowding. Destitute people 'hanging around' may be a source of tension with other groups – including other BME groups.

■ Providing information and 'myth busting'

Making information available is a critical but also controversial aspect of the integration debate. Some landlord organisations which house asylum seekers question whether established communities should be 'told' that new migrants are moving into their area – because they would not be told about other newcomers. Some have bad experiences of public meetings on the issue being taken over by racist groups.

But most practitioners interviewed in preparing this guide felt that 'preparing' the host community is a better approach – providing of course that the 'arrival' of new migrants is known in advance, and that those liaising with the community already having a trusting relationship with community representatives (eg tenants' group leaders). The approach should be 'how do we make this work?' rather than 'do you want this to happen?'.

Preparation involves supplying information, both to the host community and to the newcomers. Many organisations have produced 'myth busting' leaflets about asylum seekers (see sources in *Understanding the Stranger* and also *Tell it like it is: The truth about asylum* available at www.refugeecouncil.org.uk). These may be useful, but face-to-face contact with people is also important so that they have a chance to ask, and get answers to, their questions. As well as possible outright hostility, people may simply be poorly informed and therefore have inaccurate or prejudiced views as a result. For example in *Understanding the Stranger* a single mother is quoted as saying:

> *'Well you see them, driving their cars. With their mobile phones and clothes. And if they can't go to work, where do they get it from? We should be informed of this, if they can't go to work, where are they getting all this from?'*

The fact that NASS accommodation is often equipped with basics such as white goods may provoke local comment, if people do not realise that asylum seekers have very limited financial support.

In the Henley Green area of Coventry (see The Welcome Project in section 2), residents asked questions such as:

- why do refugees keep to themselves?
- why do they congregate in particular areas?
- how can we get opportunities to meet each other?
- why do people come to this country, why don't they stay in other countries?
- why are there so many young men?
- who is paying for what they get?

If questions like this can be anticipated (or prepared for through discussions with residents' representatives), answers can be worked out in advance. The regional consortium (where appropriate) will have information on new asylum arrivals. Organisations like ICAR (see appendix 6) can be contacted for more general help. It is a common experience that people have little idea about why refugees leave their home countries and that – once they have better information – they may be much more accepting of their presence here.

As well as the host community, new migrant groups may also need information/ advice to prepare them for the community where they are going to live. Some of the basic support mentioned in chapter 5 (like how the rubbish collection system works) is important for community relations. In Dover, asylum seekers were briefed by police on their 'rights and responsibilities' covering such issues as the law about being able to drive or that people may feel threatened by groups of young men 'hanging around'. In Bolton, local residents produced a *Guide to Bolton* for new migrants and there are also 'lifestyle mentors' – volunteers who help refugees with practical matters like accessing the internet or going to a football match.

Chapter 8 will also deal with the crucial issue of training for frontline staff (eg those dealing with general housing lettings) about how they talk about asylum seekers and other new migrants. Staff need to have the confidence and knowledge to be able to face potentially hostile questioning, and not all will be able/willing to take this on.

■ Ways of bringing people together

Levels of contact between groups can be improved both at the individual level and through local institutions. An example of the former is 'hosting' or befriending or skill-sharing schemes, which may either involve people from the established community or else older-established new migrants who have themselves developed more community links. Such schemes might focus (for example) on mothers with children, and offer practical help in making use of health and other local facilities as well as fostering personal friendships. The aim may be as much to put people in contact with other refugees (where they are not in touch already) as with longer-term residents.

Local organisations such as tenants' and residents' groups or community projects might be encouraged to make special efforts to help new migrants become members. Steps can be taken to ensure that facilities like community or sports centres are accessible and welcoming. Special 'one-off' events might be organised such as local cultural festivals or events directed at young people or through schools. Interchanges might take place between places of worship or through 'interfaith' groups.

New initiatives to understand and promote integration

Communities R Us is an initiative which aims to build a better understanding of the ways in which long-term residents and refugee communities can achieve more positive interaction. Working with refugee groups and residents' associations in three locations, the project will bring communities together to tackle a shared community concern. Hact will provide seed corn funding and ongoing support for joint activity. Models of good practice for the development of community cohesion will be identified and disseminated in the form of a toolkit.

ICAR's *Understanding the Stranger* project is to lead to a handbook of schemes which mediate tension and build bridges between long-term communities and refugees.

Contact details are in appendix 6.

■ Creating local networks

'Local networks' in this context may be networks of service providers (housing, police, schools, etc) or networks of community organisations or both – whatever seems appropriate for a particular locality. In Glasgow, for example, there are ten local networks which typically include a coordinator and representatives from the city council and statutory agencies, RCOs, voluntary organisations, faith groups, residents' organisations, etc. The evaluation study (Wren, 2004) provides useful detail on how they were set up and how they work. In Sheffield's Gleadless Valley estate (which has about 150 asylum seekers speaking 14-15 different languages), the focus has been a local 'community forum' which has a local centre with a small full-time team, a board with local residents on it, and a remit to improve the quality of life for residents generally.

Such local networks are a point of contact for those providing direct services or allocating accommodation to new migrants (eg the asylum support team placing new arrivals in an area), and offer the opportunity both to give and to receive information. Networks can be a good way of identifying gaps in local services (eg the need for interpreters) and deciding how to fill them. They can also be a way of coordinating activities aimed at bringing people in the community together and ensuring that new migrants are not left out of local events or activities. If the housing provider already has links with RCOs or other groups representing new migrants, this can be the opportunity to make sure other service providers make similar links.

In some cases, networks might be set up after change has already started to happen in an area (for example, refugees moving into local private sector accommodation) or in response to local problems such as harassment or discrimination. The catalyst might be a meeting to decide how to respond to a particular issue (eg racist incidents) or having a one-day conference of local agencies to discuss how to respond positively to the changes in an area, if possible involving representatives of new migrant groups themselves.

■ Helping people feel secure

Having a feeling of security in the home and the immediate neighbourhood is perhaps even more important for new migrants – particularly those fleeing persecution elsewhere – than it is for long-term residents. The CRE (2005) draft code of guidance on housing says that:

> *'Working closely with other local organisations, including ethnic minority community organisations, [housing organisations] should take steps to deal with security matters in all neighbourhoods, so that no one feels they must avoid certain areas. The aim should be to promote all neighbourhoods as desirable places to live for all racial groups.'*

Single refugee women are particularly vulnerable and the report *Is It Safe Here?* (Dumper, 2002) makes detailed safety recommendations, including physical alterations to accommodation.

All housing organisations should, as part of their race equality work, have policies and practices in place to tackle racist harassment. In adapting these to the circumstances of new migrant groups, they need to review their procedures, check if new approaches are needed and make sure preventative measures are in place.

Reviewing procedures

This guide is not the place to review in detail the approaches that might be taken. There is guidance available from CIH, from the Home Office (including NASS guidance), the police service and through resources such as www.raceactionnet. co.uk. Some of the more general guidance on tackling anti-social behaviour is also relevant. Among other issues, local policies and practices should:

- have a clear definition of harassment, including examples that refer to new migrant groups
- put appropriate requirements into tenancy agreements, and get the support of tenants' groups for them
- include comprehensive procedures on reporting incidents
- provide support for victims (including measures such as 24-hour panic alarms); provide for positive support for groups such as newly-housed asylum seekers or other newcomers who might be more vulnerable
- have measures for dealing with perpetrators
- be based on effective and committed multi-agency working (housing, police, schools, etc)

- allow for monitoring so that new patterns of racist harassment (eg against new migrant groups) can be identified
- build in preventative measures.

Evaluating the need for new approaches
Depending on the severity or pattern of incidents, it might be decided to adopt new approaches such as having a dedicated agency, creating special training programmes for staff involved, working directly with local schools, etc. One issue (for example) may be that support to victims, originally offered to established minority groups in English, might now have to be made available in other languages because of changes in who is coming to live in an area.

Taking preventative measures
Exchange of information might itself be a good preventative measure, as might other activities mentioned earlier. Measures to deal with perpetrators – including restorative justice approaches (eg workshops with offenders) and/or anti-social behaviour orders – may also be relevant. Coventry has a 'hate crime campaign' as an integral part of the city's Crime Reduction Partnership. A recent study (Lemos, 2005) on challenging racist attitudes among young people gives several practical examples (one is cited in section 2). Refugee Action is running a refugee awareness project in three cities, aimed at changing local perceptions.

Anticipating potential problems (through the medium of local networks mentioned earlier) can be important. In Waltham Forest, for example, an interagency group was set up to consider how to deal with community conflicts thought likely in the build up to the Iraq war in 2003.

■ Changing perceptions more widely

Obviously, local perceptions are at least as affected by such wider factors as political debates and media treatment of asylum seekers as they are about what actually happens locally. This guide does not address the issue of national campaigning, but at local level there is scope for addressing problems like inaccurate press reporting or the poor 'image' of asylum seekers. Three areas are addressed here: political commitment, local media liaison and positive expression of an alternative viewpoint through local exhibitions, libraries, etc.

Political commitment
While at local level it is difficult to enter the national political debate, there is much that can be done to ensure that council members, housing association board members, tenant leaders and local MPs are politically committed to housing and supporting new migrant groups. For example:

- cross-party political agreement can be sought to a 'refugee housing strategy' or other key elements of this work – in Sheffield there is a cross-party group at cabinet level which agrees key issues such as the council's commitment to the Gateway programme (see page 19)

- MPs and other politicians can be invited to see positive examples of the contribution new migrants can make – for example, in making local schools more viable and/or improving school exam results
- campaigns to 'save' asylum seekers whose cases have been rejected can be used to broaden the argument and educate local representatives, the media, etc about the issues.

Local media liaison

An ICAR study (2004) showed the impact which unbalanced media coverage can have on local attitudes, and that it may even be linked directly to racist harassment. In cities which have large numbers of new migrants, such as Glasgow, Sheffield and Leicester, liaison with local media has helped to improve coverage. For example, local newspaper editors might agree not to print racist letters and might be willing to give coverage to local 'success stories' involving new migrants. Various resources exist on media issues:

- The Refugee Council website has advice on writing to the press and guidelines which the press should be following.
- The MediaWise Trust (www.presswise.org.uk) argues for responsible reporting, and has advice on refugees and the media.
- The RAM Project (www.ramproject.org.uk) has recently published (2005) a report on how to improve media coverage; papers such as the *Bristol Evening Post* have welcomed the praise that RAM gave them.
- IPPR have published (2005) *Seeking Scapegoats – The coverage of asylum in the UK press* (www.ippr.org).
- The issue is also covered in government guidance on community cohesion (www.communitycohesion.gov.uk).

The Yorkshire and Humberside Consortium has a media strategy which is periodically updated. Some of its principles are:

- break significant stories to the local rather than national media (which often do not care about the consequences of their reports)
- avoid preaching or polemic
- tell the truth, in as sensitive way as you can
- let your contacts hear about things from you first.

Creating a positive image for new migrants

Taking the message directly to local communities can often be a productive approach. For example, Sheffield City Council has a mobile exhibition (called *Moving Here*) aimed at telling the true story about asylum to young people, which has been very popular (www.sheffield.gov.uk/education/lea-services/emas). Leicester's Amity group (amitymedia@hotmail.com) publishes the magazine *Alive* which is written partly by refugees and promotes positive news stories of new migrants generally. The BBC has a local radio project aimed at finding and celebrating 'world musicians' living in British cities such as Leeds (www.bbc. co.uk/radio3/world/onyourstreet/index.shtml). Many organisations use 'Refugee Week' in June each year as a focus for local events to promote understanding of refugees. This may be the opportunity to link current conflicts (such as, at the time or writing, Darfur in Sudan) with people who have taken refuge here.

■

Section 2: Practical Examples

❏ Improving personal understanding between people

Some of the practical examples in earlier chapters, such as Charter HA's Learning Links project in Newport (see page 69) or the Praxis Hosting Scheme (see page 42), are also aimed at improving understanding between people. Leicester's Northfields Estate provides an example of successful involvement of a residents' association prior to the arrival of new migrants in an area.

Practical example
A residents' association welcomes new migrants

Northfields was a declining estate and Leicester City Council wanted to attract people to the area. It worked with the tenants' and residents' association (TARA) to consider ideas about improving the sustainability of the estate and increasing demand for the housing. This resulted in groups of both asylum seekers and new Somali migrants from other EU countries moving into the estate, but only after 12 months preparatory work in which the TARA played a vital role. Meetings were held at which people were able to voice their concerns, and people from new migrant communities in other parts of the city were invited to help allay peoples' concerns. When new tenants started to arrive, housing staff introduced them to their neighbours three doors on either side to help them get to know each other. Measures were taken to improve life on the estate generally, for example by more vigorously tackling anti-social behaviour, and these were seen as benefiting all residents not just newcomers.

More details: Robinson (2004), pp 40-45.

❏ Providing information and 'myth busting'

A further example of working with residents is provided by Coventry's Welcome Project, which started in an area where the number of new migrants has already grown over the last few years.

Practical example
Better informing local residents

The Welcome Project, in which local Coventry agencies are working with ICAR to follow up lessons from *Understanding the Stranger*, focuses initially on the north-east of the city, where there has been an influx both of refugees and of new migrants from other EU countries. The project has five stages – information gathering, assessing residents' and new migrants' concerns through focus groups, training for frontline staff, developing a range of local events, activities or resources to respond to the issues that emerge, and finally a learning/dissemination stage.

The project, financed through the Neighbourhood Renewal Fund, began in February 2004. Contacts have been made with residents' and refugee groups and an early focus has been on 'myth busting'.

More details: barbara.hall@coventry-refugee-centre.org

Providing information to new migrants can also be a means of stimulating new contacts, as happened in Pennywell, Sunderland.

Practical example
Local residents provide practical help for newcomers

Pennywell in Sunderland is an area where asylum seekers have been housed, and prior to this Sunderland Housing briefed the local residents' association who were keen to help. Gladys Chilton, a residents' association member, decided to meet asylum seekers as they arrived, introduce them to neighbours, take them to shops and the post office – and challenge any negative reactions they encountered. She has been the coordinator for local social events such as 'singing nights' which have been popular with long-term residents as well as newcomers. The result is reportedly that many asylum seekers now feel part of the local community.

More details: info@sunderlandhousinggroup.co.uk.org

An example of a 'myth busting' leaflet comes from Northern Ireland.

Practical example
Local 'myth busting' leaflet

Northern Ireland's Refugee Action group has published a leaflet called *Forced to Flee* which captures the reader's interest by setting images and personal stories about asylum seekers alongside answers to frequently asked questions. These include answers specific to the area, such as why asylum seekers are imprisoned and whether Northern Ireland is a 'soft touch'.

Downloadable from: www.amnesty.org.uk/ni

❑ Ways of bringing people together

Two projects aimed at reducing the social isolation that refugees often feel have focussed – respectively – on women with children and on young unaccompanied refugees.

Practical example
Local residents provide practical help for families

Sure Start Friends is a home visiting and befriending scheme in Foleshill, Coventry, for asylum seekers and refugees. Volunteers, who receive training, are (so far) all women, and many are also refugees. They befriend families referred to the project from midwives, doctors, the local refugee centre, etc, visiting them during the daytime, 'signposting' them to local facilities and offering other basic support. Some of the volunteers speak minority languages. Currently there are ten families involved in the scheme and 22 volunteers. Both 'sides' benefit because the volunteers get valuable training and experience which helps them in looking for jobs – ten previous volunteers now have paid employment. The project is funded through Sure Start.

More details: 024 7666 1631

Practical example
Providing a social centre for young refugees

SOVA in partnership with Cardiff Children Services used the Home Office Challenge Fund to set up a drop-in centre for young unaccompanied refugees and their peer mentors.

Young refugees were referred to the drop-in centre primarily by social workers. Ten volunteer 'peer mentors' were recruited (and then trained) through the education department, Cardiff Children Services, etc. They all either had experience of living in care or of life as an immigrant. The Welsh Refugee Council provided premises, free of charge, and further support was received from various organisations.

The challenge was to establish a drop-in centre with a friendly, safe atmosphere and to create enjoyable activities. The centre aimed to help young people emerge from their feelings of isolation and have somewhere safe to mix with other young people with similar experiences. The mix of ethnic groups encouraged confidence and broke down barriers.

The centre helped young people to develop their language skills, with two hours of ESOL training weekly. Day trips to places such as Cardiff Bay and London helped orientate young people to Cardiff and experience the culture of the UK. Some 33 young refugees visited the centre. The self-evaluation report for the Home Office identifies successful practices developed, so that other organisations can continue these initiatives as the project does not have continuing finance.

More details: www.sova.org.uk

❑ Creating local networks

An example of an approach to forming a local network is being funded in Birmingham through hact's Accommodate project.

Practical example in development
Forming a local network

Housing agencies in north-west Birmingham (a Housing Market Renewal Pathfinder) identified the need to achieve better coordination of their services to refugees in an area where many refugees are already living. The project (which is in the early stages) aims to bring together several housing associations and work to establish or improve their links with local RCOs. One of the members of the network is a local housing resource centre which already has experience of giving advice to refugees and working with RCOs. The need for the project emerged partly from a research study into local refugee housing needs, and the deficiencies in housing and support services. One aim is to ensure that refugees benefit from the pathfinder work.

More details: 0121 766 5115

❑ Helping people feel secure

Practical example
Sharing experiences helps to counteract effects of harassment

Manchester's Routes project is financed by Manchester Children's Fund. It supports asylum seeking and other migrant women and families, giving practical help and support to those who have experienced racial harassment. Shabana Baig, a caseworker with Routes, says they have worked with women from Pakistan, Africa and previously from the Czech Republic. Many children of asylum seekers are high achievers at school, she says:

> *'Routes tries to empower people, help them to be stronger and confident in dealing with the different systems they have to face and their new life in this country. There's no point in us doing everything for them and not allowing them to learn and develop themselves in order to cope better here. For some people, just knowing one person they can turn to who will help them is so important amidst all the uncertainty they are faced with.'* The Guardian, 4 January 2005

The project has been evaluated by the National Evaluation of the Children's Fund.

More details: 0161 853 3393

Practical example
Challenging racism among young people

Peterborough's You, Me and Us programme is run with young people in all the city's high schools. It is an intensive, one day programme aimed at 'challenging prejudice and hatred wherever it is found'. A recent study tracked students' attitudes before and after they experienced the programme. It found extensive, if minority, dislike of certain ethnic groups, and feelings that there were 'too many' racial groups in the city. The evaluation after the groups had experienced the programme revealed that more than 70 percent felt differently about racism as a result of it.

More details: Lemos, G (2005), pp 15-32.

❏ Changing perceptions more widely

The Refugee Media Group in Wales has published a practical guide to dealing with media issues, aimed particularly at RCOs or other local groups.

Practical example
Dealing with the media

This downloadable guide is a source of information on tackling media issues, and includes 'grassroots' experience from Wales, advice on using the stories of refugees themselves, what to do in interviews, and guidance on interviewing women refugees. It has several 'what worked for us' sections that are particularly useful for local groups.

More details: www.cardiff.ac.uk/jomec/en/centres/96.html

Students in Manchester produced a video which helped to overcome doubts and myths about asylum seekers.

Practical example
Citizenship project tackles asylum issues

Students at Manchester's Lostosk High School made the video which now forms part of a touring exhibition called *Terminal Frontiers*. The video, *Alem will stay*, shows students arguing over the fate of Alem, a fictional asylum seeker due to be deported. The project began when the school started to take asylum seekers as students, as part of the process of countering misinformation and racist attitudes on the part of existing students. Staff realised that students needed to engage with the issues at the human level, and based the fictional case on a story in a book by Benjamin Zephaniah, from which the drama was developed.

More details: www.virtualmigrants.com

Checklist on living in a community

✓ is someone 'in charge' of integration and community cohesion issues in your area (responsible for identifying problems and bringing people together to work out solutions)?

✓ are you familiar with statutory requirements and guidance, and the expectations of regulators on these issues?

✓ are there parts of your area where a 'community support plan' is needed?

✓ what other organisations, local agencies and residents' groups will you need to work with if the plan is to be effective?

✓ how will you go about deciding what issues and priorities there are locally?

✓ what measures will you take to make sure you get the views of all groups in the area, not just those who 'shout the loudest'?

✓ how effectively does your organisation respond to community tensions and racist incidents involving new migrants?

✓ is the response rapid? – and can you count on the support of other agencies like the police?

Chapter 7

Working in Partnership

What this chapter is about

- why partnership working is important
- refugee community organisations
- local partnerships
- regional-level organisations
- national organisations

This guide aims to encourage housing bodies to do more to ensure that asylum seekers, refugees and other new migrants have good accommodation and proper services. But it also recognises that, while housing providers can often be the catalyst, they will usually need partnerships with other bodies to secure better services. This is because other organisations have necessary expertise, because the range of support services needed (see chapter 5) is so wide that no single body is likely to be able to provide them all, and also because of the need to 'join up' services and try to close any gaps. In practice, in any area, there is likely to be a patchwork of services already in place, and it will make sense to engage with bodies providing them to identify unmet needs and develop a strategy for meeting them.

This chapter starts by looking at partnership working in principle. It offers guidance on relationships with bodies representative of refugees and other new migrants, then looks at other local organisations, private landlords, regional bodies and national bodies that housing practitioners are likely to need to contact.

❏ Principles of partnership working

As said earlier, partnership working is fundamental to the kind of support services considered in this guide. However, it is not the place to go into detail on how to go about setting up and working in partnerships, as there is extensive guidance on this, including guidance on housing-related support services. For example, *Crossing the Housing and Care Divide: A guide for practitioners* (Marsh, 2005) has detailed material on setting up partnerships and initiating joint projects. The website www.renewal.net has toolkits on partnerships and related issues.

Some of the principles involved can be summarised, however.

First, reasons for seeking partnerships (such as those mentioned) have to be considered in relation to the situation in a particular area. 'Partnerships' are not necessarily always the answer, and do require a lot of effort. Organisations therefore need to be clear about their reasons and their aims.

Second, especially if this is a new area of service provision, it is important to 'map' which bodies have an interest in this area of work and may be interested in joint working. For example, some agencies may already work with refugees or other new migrants, may be involved in referring them, or may have experience of working with them elsewhere.

Third, in considering setting up partnerships, you will need to bear in mind any agencies with which your organisation already has working relationships, and how to approach other agencies which are not familiar to you. Can you offer them something which will make a partnership potentially attractive, such as helping them with a problem (eg lack of interpretation services) which they may have? Can you do some background work to 'learn their language' so that your proposals to them will appear sensible and to relate to their concerns?

Fourth, in getting a partnership off the ground, try to involve potential partners from the outset and develop shared aims for what you are doing. Have some ideas about the management and funding of services that are envisaged, and how they might be evaluated. It will be useful if someone who has the time and skills is willing to 'take the lead' to see the project through.

Fifth, give some thought to how the service or project will be 'kept on track' so that it really meets the needs of potential users and makes effective use of resources. Consider how service users might be involved, and how the effectiveness of the service can be monitored in relation to the different sources of funding which may be employed.

If your organisation already knows about or has relationships with refugee or other new migrant groups (see below), this will give it a considerable advantage in establishing new partnerships.

❑ Working with refugee community organisations (RCOs)

'Refugee community organisation' means a body run by refugees and acting on behalf or providing services for refugees. They range from informal groups that are just getting going to long-established ones with full-time staff.

Many RCOs serve particular national or ethnic groups (Somalis, Kurds, etc). Some of the longest-established RCOs now offer housing accommodation, and these are often known as Refugee Community Housing Associations (RCHAs), although only a few are formally 'registered' associations. Many RCOs and RCHAs also represent – and may provide services to – asylum seekers. Other new migrant groups also have community organisations, but this chapter refers only to RCOs or RCHAs – although the points made have general relevance to other migrant groups.

■ Helping RCOs to develop

Most RCOs have developed through groups of refugees getting together to tackle problems – and housing problems are often at the forefront. Those who take the lead may be accepted refugees or settled residents – perhaps from a particular national or ethnic group where newcomers are still arriving in Britain. In large cities there may be several RCOs at various stages of development – the most advanced already providing services like those mentioned in earlier chapters.

How can a local authority or housing association help emerging RCOs? First they have to be identified, which can be done by talking to new migrants themselves and finding out if they know about individuals or groups within their community to whom they can turn for help. Second, it is useful to meet with the groups, find out what they are doing and what their aims are, and what help they might need. Some examples of the kind of help that it might be possible to offer are:

- rooms for meetings
- help towards administrative or publicity costs
- help with devising a constitution
- contacts with similar, more advanced groups who are willing to share their experiences
- help with applying for project funding.

South London Family HA appointed a link officer for a year to work with an RCO with which it was building a relationship.

It is in the interests of housing organisations that there are RCOs to which they can relate and which can provide a means of communication with new migrants as service users, just as housing organisations would encourage the formation of tenants' groups in areas which do not have them.

In some cases there may be no 'critical mass' to enable an RCO to emerge – too few people in a particular community to support one. In these cases it would be appropriate to maintain contact with individuals and set up interim consultation arrangements from which an RCO might later develop.

While it may be difficult for an emerging RCO to show that it is representative, it is useful to have some basic criteria against which to judge whether to support a new RCO. For example, the Scottish Refugee Council (SRC) has tests such as the group being non-sectarian, operating within the law, and not marginalising women. Subject to such tests, emerging RCOs may be helped by the SRC and Glasgow City Council's *Framework for Dialogue*, which promotes refugee participation in local services, helps contact between newcomers and RCOs, and between RCOs representing different communities.

■ Working with new RCOs

Once a group is established, ideally it should have regular contact with housing organisations providing services and with whichever department or body is taking the lead on the overall strategy for support services and integration. It is likely to want both to raise and influence policy issues, and have a means of pursuing individual cases presented to it. At the same time RCOs provide housing organisations with information on the nature and extent of needs and their experience can help in the development of culturally-sensitive services.

Examples of the kinds of relationship that might develop with new RCOs are:

- RCOs carrying out informal needs surveys among the groups they represent
- housing organisations training RCO members involved in giving advice, so that they understand how lettings, homelessness practices, housing benefit and so on work
- involving RCOs in refugee forums which bring together statutory, non-statutory and voluntary or community groups to discuss problems and services, and possibly to devise strategies (see chapter 9).

If RCOs can move towards providing *support services*, not just advice, this is both good in itself and offers the possibility of longer-term funding and stability. RCOs also have a clear potential role in promoting community cohesion – several of the Accommodate projects (see below), and others mentioned in chapter 6, involve RCOs. Often, however, an RCO is in a 'chicken and egg' position – it needs to grow in order to have the capacity to provide wider services, but to grow it needs the income that such services would deliver. Housing organisations may be able to help RCOs build their capacity and overcome these 'growing pains'.

■ Working with established RCOs

Longer-established RCOs may well have some full or part-time staff and already be engaged in service provision. Such RCOs may:

- be innovative and developing good practice
- use a 'holistic' approach to working with refugees, covering a range of different needs and acting as intermediaries with statutory services

- provide services in a safe, friendly environment that takes account of cultural and language needs
- concentrate on advice work initially, and may venture into housing provision (see below) in response to demand
- show considerable commitment, especially where there is a sole member of staff doing many different tasks
- are able to provide services (eg helping destitute people) that official agencies find difficult or are not allowed to fund.

RCOs interviewed for this guide found it difficult to say how they could demonstrate that they are 'representative,' because they often rely on informal networks. However, they believed that they were open to all, had representative boards or trustees, and that a key test was their reputation and the extent to which their target groups used their services.

Among the difficulties RCOs face in their work are:
- insecurity of funding (which may be an – inappropriate – motive to become a landlord)
- funding often being tied to projects so that 'core' funding is not available to assist the RCO's general work
- lack of capacity or skills in making funding applications and/or severe competition for funds
- lack of understanding by potential funders of how RCOs operate
- establishing positive relationships – with local authorities and housing associations – in which the RCO is seen as a partner not a client
- finding suitable accommodation for clients and dealing with housing benefit and other financial issues
- being unable to cope with the demands of destitute people
- dealing with the current limited availability of legal aid (see chapter 5).

It is a common demand that established RCOs want the same kind of 'partner' status with local authorities or housing associations as might apply to other well-established voluntary sector groups. By establishing a person or team with specific responsibility for RCO liaison, the LA or HA can help to shape such a relationship and get full benefit from the experience which RCOs can offer.

■ Working with RCHAs

RCHAs are usually longer-established organisations, many London-based, which have decided to meet housing needs directly by becoming landlords. Some have become significant organisations – for example, Afro-Caribbean HA was established in 1994, has 100 properties in nine London boroughs, and a turnover exceeding £1 million.

Normally RCHA accommodation is leased from the private sector (sometimes from owners from the same ethnic community), from housing associations or in some cases empty/derelict council property which is renovated (see page 43). Their strengths are similar to RCOs (see above) with the added element of aiming to provide a culturally-sensitive landlord service.

The additional difficulties which RCHAs face include:

- developing the capacity to deal with property management – a complex area of work which cannot be taken on without adequate resources
- perceptions by HAs that business with RCHAs is high risk or time-consuming (because of the type of property and client group, and lack of management capacity)
- difficulty in making contacts at sufficiently high levels with larger HAs
- shortage of properties – especially in London
- need for staff training in housing management – which some have now addressed
- their committee's unfamiliarity with housing management issues, leading to conflict over the handling of cases.

RCHAs have little prospect of (or may not want) registered landlord status, yet want to build their landlord role. Many would like to establish stronger partnerships with social landlords and to diversify their property portfolios. Some do have strong relationships already. RCHAs perceive themselves as different from most of the recognised BME housing associations (see below) and often find it difficult to establish relationships either with them or with mainstream associations. Given pressures of housing demand, however, they have a vital role in helping a client group which is otherwise heavily dependent on the private sector.

❏ Local partnerships

Readers of this guide are likely to be working in either local authorities or housing associations and thinking about local-level partnerships for providing services. A local authority housing department may want to make links with other departments and with housing associations either already working locally or who may have expertise to offer. A housing association will want to work in collaboration with relevant local authorities and possibly with other associations. Here are some of the possible organisational links to bear in mind, with some examples of joint working already taking place.

■ Strategic partnerships

Strategic partnerships are groups of organisations working together to deliver a strategy. In some places (eg Leicester), accommodation has been the starting point for developing a strategy, so the council's housing department took the lead in creating the partnership. In others (eg Sheffield Refugee Forum/City Council's *New Lives: Refugee Integration Strategy 2005-2008*), the partnership itself took the lead. Whichever is the case, housing, social services and education departments are certain to be involved.

Outside the local authority, bodies such as the Primary Care Trusts, police, adult education providers and other housing providers are likely to be partners – together with the local translation/interpreter service, if there is one. Local representatives of national bodies (see below) are also likely to have services that contribute. Established RCOs (see above) should be included both as groups representative of new migrants and/or as actual or potential service providers.

One approach to strategic partnerships is to use existing arrangements instead of forming new ones. Many local authorities have local strategic partnerships (community planning partnerships in Scotland), community strategies or other coordinating arrangements to bring agencies together. This can work as a way of getting overall commitment, but the actual strategy is likely to need more detailed, lower-level collaboration.

■ Service providers

> '*We want to remind housing associations that it is good business to get involved in refugee housing.*'
> Jon Rouse, Chief Executive of the Housing Corporation, 24 June 2004.

As seen in chapters 4 and 5, there are likely to be many different providers of housing and support services in any one area, including public sector bodies, independent but accountable bodies such as housing associations, and voluntary sector organisations including RCOs. Some housing associations have particular expertise:

- Specialist housing associations such as RHA and ARHAG have lengthy experience of delivering accommodation and support services.
- Safe Haven Yorkshire, a company established by two HAs (South Yorkshire HA and Yorkshire Housing Group) has a specialist role in delivering NASS contracts in Yorkshire and Humberside, catering for about 3,000 asylum seekers with a staff of 120 (nearly half of whom are from BME groups, speaking 50 languages).
- Some medium or larger associations (such as Focus Group) have experience of providing accommodation and services – see examples in chapter 4.
- Others support local RCOs or RCHAs by providing facilities, training or leased accommodation.
- Some associations which are care specialists (such as Bournemouth Churches HA – see chapter 5) have developed expertise in refugee support.
- Stock transfer has led new associations in (for example) Bradford and Coventry to develop services for asylum seekers and refugees.

- BME housing associations (that is, ones where at least 80 percent of board members are from BME groups), already have experience of providing culturally-sensitive services and may be interested in expanding these to new migrant groups. (The box discusses the potential of BME HAs generally, based partly on material collected by FBHO.)

Actual and potential contribution of BME housing associations

There are 64 registered BME housing associations in England, around half of which own less than 200 properties, although three larger London-based ones together own or manage more than 8,000 units. BME associations are largely based in London and other big cities. Most are relatively young organisations set up in the 1980s with their base in the long-established BME communities in the cities where they originated.

A recent report *The Future of BME Housing Associations* (Lupton and Perry, 2004) looked at the potential areas of work in which these associations are engaged or might be engaged in future. Some like Ashiana HA in Rochdale are already involved in community cohesion initiatives. Others like Manningham HA in Bradford have started working with refugee groups. The report recognised that while BME associations may not have relationships with newly-emerging migrant communities, they are potentially well-placed to understand their needs and help in providing culturally-sensitive services. However, as the report said, 'there is a reputation to be built' by established BME associations among refugee communities, an opinion reflected in discussions with RCOs for this guide.

Ways in which BME associations might work with new migrant groups include (with current examples):
- providing accommodation (Nashayman HA, a BME association in Yorkshire, is providing units for letting to asylum seekers)
- providing accommodation and support (ASRA Greater London has a unit for homelessness families in Camden which supports refugees and other newcomers, using their experience of delivering culturally-sensitive services and linking with two local RCOs and a RCHA)
- using their expertise in developing culturally-sensitive services to help others do so (Ashram HA, part of the Accord Group, offers the rest of the group its expertise in areas of race and cultural diversity; another group member, BCHS, has started a project managing refugee accommodation – see page 44)
- widening their experience of community cohesion to work with new migrant communities (Manningham HA is leading the Bradford Accommodate project and will use its experience in integration work with long-established BME groups which have moved to areas with few BME people)
- becoming representative of refugees in a wider sense (ARHAG is a refugee-oriented BME association which has a range of initiatives such as a tenant empowerment project which combines training in use of new technology with improved communication between ARHAG and tenants)

■ Private landlords

Private renting provides one of the main routes by which new migrants get housing. Landlords may simply let individual properties or places in multi-occupied properties to new migrants, as they would to anyone else. Landlords may lease properties to RCHAs or other organisations, which then let them to refugees (see examples in chapter 4). Or they may have a NASS contract, as do companies like Clearsprings and Adelphi Hotels. These larger landlords with experience of accommodating asylum seekers often actively collaborate in local partnerships.

❑ English regional organisations

■ Regional consortia

Regional consortia are the bodies representing and coordinating stakeholders and service providers engaged in the NASS programme. They liaise with NASS at regional level, negotiate and oversee accommodation and support contracts within the region, and have a role in refugee integration and promoting RCOs. They are funded partly by local authorities and partly through NASS and other sources.

The National Consortia Support Team, based in Leeds, supports the regional consortia and also those in Wales and Scotland. It publishes a regular bulletin (available at www.refugeeaccess.info).

■ Other regional bodies

Regional development agencies are responsible for wider economic development at regional level and (currently) regional housing boards are responsible for regional housing strategy. Policy issues concerning new migrant groups clearly exist at regional level, but so far there has been little engagement in them. The consortia have a role in putting pressure on and supplying information and ideas to these bodies.

❑ Scotland, Wales and Northern Ireland

The Scottish Executive and Welsh Assembly Government have taken an active interest in new migration issues. Although responsibility for policy and legislation is not devolved, in practice both have been encouraged by the Home Office to develop refugee integration policies. The Scottish Refugee Integration Forum has recently updated its *Action Plan* on refugee integration (SRIF, 2005). The Scottish Executive also has a prominent Fresh Talent programme of encouraging more migration to Scotland, showing the positive economic contribution new migrants make and – to some extent – changing public and media attitudes. The Welsh Assembly Government (2005) has published guidance on housing and related services and is developing a 'refugee inclusion strategy'.

In both Scotland and Wales there are consortia similar to those in England (see above). The Scottish consortium is coordinated by COSLA (website details in appendix 6). The Welsh consortium does not have an accommodation contract but is funded by the Home Office to improve service access for asylum seekers.

In Northern Ireland there has been less active engagement, possibly in part because there is no 'dispersal' of asylum seekers and because of low overall numbers. There are, however, significant numbers of migrants from other EU countries in low paid jobs (see page 35).

❏ Bodies at UK level

■ Government bodies

The Home Office is responsible for migration law, policy and administration across the UK. One division of the Home Office, the Immigration and Nationality Directorate (IND), has overall responsibility for policy and for administering the immigration system (at ports of entry, etc). NASS is a directorate within IND and has offices at regional level and in Glasgow, Cardiff and Belfast (see appendix 4 for current developments in NASS).

Other parts of the Home Office deal with community cohesion, refugee integration, race relations, the police, crime prevention and other policy and operational issues relevant to this guide. Some of these are UK-wide and some relate only to England.

Housing policy and community regeneration are dealt with separately for England and the three devolved administrations. ODPM (in England) has until recently not treated refugee or new migrant housing issues as especially important, probably because the Home Office is seen as having the lead role. For example, IND has a National Refugee Integration Forum (NRIF) which has an accommodation sub-group dealing with housing and related issues, on which national bodies like CIH and NHF are represented and to which housing practitioners contribute. ODPM takes part in this.

IND also convenes a National Asylum Support Forum (NASF) which has wide-ranging representation including RCOs, and deals with issues such the links between NASS and mainstream housing provision. The Home Office and ODPM have (in 2005) a jointly-seconded housing practitioner working on tackling refugee homelessness.

The Housing Corporation is encouraging English housing associations to engage with refugee housing provision, and has recently published the report *Still Surviving and Now Settling* (Zetter, 2005) which follows up earlier work in this area and shows how HAs might be more involved. Its affordable housing programme for 2006/08 encourages refugee support schemes and engagement with RCOs.

■ Non-government bodies

It is impossible to list or do justice to the range of bodies at national level working in this field. These are some of the ones most relevant from a housing viewpoint and which have local-level projects or services (for these and other contact details, see appendix 6):

- *The Refugee Council* develops policy, gives practical guidance, offers a range of services for asylum seekers, refugees and RCOs, and has regional offices in the Midlands, East Anglia and Yorkshire. The *Scottish Refugee Council* and *Welsh Refugee Council* have similar roles.

- *Refugee Action* is both a campaign body and a service provider (in England), working through its regional offices in areas such as Bolton and Leicester.

- *Hact* has a range of programmes concerning refugee housing and integration and publishes research and good practice material. Its Accommodate programme is working in five areas in England and hact has a project looking at good practice among housing providers in Wales.

- *ICAR* is a UK-wide information and research centre, with a range of practical information and programmes on all refugee-related issues. It has a number of projects with local connections (eg in Coventry).

- The *Empty Homes Agency* promotes active use of empty properties and has helped RCOs and others make use of them for refugee accommodation.

- *Positive Action in Housing* is an ethnic minority-led charity campaigning and offering advice on refugee housing issues in Scotland.

- *Northern Ireland Council for Ethnic Minorities* runs support services for asylum seekers and campaigns on refugee issues.

In addition, many of the national programmes mentioned in the practical examples in earlier chapters (Sova, Sure Start, Rainer, Connexions, etc) are involved in providing local support services.

Checklist on partnership working

✓ are there any partnership arrangements for working with refugees or new migrant groups in your area?

✓ is there a need for them?

✓ what organisations might need to be involved?

✓ who knows about and has contact with refugee community organisations?

✓ could more be done to support RCOs, or encourage them to form if they don't already exist?

✓ what role might they play in providing services?

✓ are there organisations which already have expertise in working with new migrant groups, perhaps in other parts of the country, who can make a contribution?

✓ are there BME housing associations who might be interested in this area of work?

✓ are you familiar with and do you have contact with the relevant national organisations working with refugees and new migrants?

CHAPTER 8

RESOURCES

What this chapter is about

- the different kinds of resources needed
- funding sources – mainstream
- funding sources – others
- staff skills
- information

Improved services for new migrants are bound to need resources of various kinds – finance, people and information. This chapter deals with the resources available to or which could be sought by a housing organisation itself. The previous chapter, on partnerships, covered the possibilities for links with other bodies in order to develop or improve services.

The chapter is mainly concerned with 'official' resources, bearing in mind that the most important resource in assisting new migrants is other new migrants – people who have been through the system and 'know the ropes'. This resource can be tapped through RCOs (see previous chapter) and of course through recruitment. Many organisations working successfully with refugees are doing so (in part) because they have refugees working with *them* – as staff, volunteers or on management committees.

❏ Funding

In considering sources of finance for new or improved services, an important aim should be to secure permanent funding as soon as it is apparent that a service is needed on a long-term basis. One of the problems that most affects support services for new migrants is temporary funding for projects for which there is long-term need. 'Seed corn' funding does of course enable new ideas to be tested out and new services to prove themselves before getting mainstream funding. But ongoing reliance on short-term grants causes various problems:

- uncertainty
- energy devoted to fund-raising instead of providing services
- difficulty in building expertise when staff are temporary or insecure
- competition for funding between projects
- pressure to 'innovate' or establish new projects even when there is an established need for an already-existing service.

The aim should be to secure permanent funding as soon as can reasonably be expected, and to persuade partner organisations providing complementary services to take the same approach, and fund services from mainstream budgets.

■ Mainstream housing funding

This section deals with funding sources available generally to housing organisations, giving brief examples. It is a complex topic and detailed guidance is available elsewhere.

Capital funding

Finance for buildings (whether new or converted) comes from borrowing, which may be supported by revenue subsidy for local authorities, or by capital grant for housing associations. Either can supplement such borrowing from their own resources, such as capital receipts (local authorities) or reserves (associations). For a local authority, whether capital expenditure is financed from the Housing Revenue Account (HRA) (through rents and subsidy) or from the General Fund (through Revenue Support Grant) depends on the client-group. For example, a hostel for homeless refugees may be a General Fund project while permanent housing would be HRA-funded.

Revenue funding

Finance for running costs (staff, services, etc) comes from revenue – in the case of local authorities, again either HRA or General Fund depending whether the clients are council tenants or not. Some councils have a special budget within their General Fund for voluntary sector initiatives – this can be useful for getting new projects like an advice centre off the ground or for sponsoring a new group such as an RCO. Some housing associations have funds for community-led initiatives (eg Refugee HA supports refugee-related projects in areas where is it working).

Supporting People (SP)

The mainstream revenue funding for support services, whether to council tenants or any other group, is now the government's Supporting People fund – allocated to local level on an annual basis. This means that, for example, a new floating support service for refugees will have to compete for finance with other needs groups such as people with learning difficulties, at a time when overall budgets are restricted. On the other hand, SP is a potential source of long-term funding for refugee support, providing the particular need is accepted as part of the local SP strategy.

Accommodation-related Home Office funding

Housing bodies with NASS contracts receive Home Office funding, and social services authorities receive payments for unaccompanied children. These payment streams may provide capacity to fund wider support/integration work. NASS also pays enabling grant to regional consortia to assist with wider liaison and service development work. Authorities which take part in initiatives such as the Gateway programme (see chapter 3) also receive direct funding.

Neighbourhood regeneration

The ODPM and the devolved administrations have various funds for neighbourhood renewal or tackling social exclusion, which might be appropriate for new migrant services or for neighbourhoods where new migrants live. For example, the ODPM's annual Neighbourhood Renewal Fund is directed at the 88 most deprived areas – many of which will in practice accommodate new migrants. Similar programmes are the Community Regeneration Fund (Scotland) and the Communities First programme (Wales). Wales also has the associated Communities First Trust Fund for associated, small-scale projects by local groups. Northern Ireland's Department for Social Development (www.dsdni.gov.uk) has funding programmes to support voluntary and community groups and urban regeneration.

Housing-related community initiatives

Funds exist for new community-based projects, especially those which demonstrate innovation in some way and/or are aimed at promoting community cohesion. Examples are:

- *Innovation and Good Practice (IGP)* and Community Enabling and Training grants from the Housing Corporation (contact 0845 230 7000).

- *Innovation into Action* grants for projects involving council tenants in England (check www.innovationintoaction.org for future availability of funds).

- *Social Housing Management Grant* fulfils a similar role in Wales (details: Grants@wales.gsi.gov.uk).

- *Communities Scotland* has a wide range of grant funds for regeneration or community initiatives, potentially suitable for new migrant projects – for example, the New Ideas Fund, Scottish Community Action Research Fund, Seeing is Believing fund and Futurebuilders Scotland (www.communitiesscotland.gov.uk, section on 'grants'). One that may be particularly useful is HomePoint grant to develop housing information or advice services.

Other initiatives

Government initiatives to tackle issues such as homelessness or anti-social behaviour may be appropriate for projects assisting new migrants or addressing community conflicts. Funding tends to reflect current priorities – for example, the Welsh Assembly Government has 'section 180' grants for homelessness projects involving voluntary groups – one has been used for a 'bond scheme' to facilitate access to private rented accommodation (see page 34) . Communities Scotland has a small Special Needs Capital Grant fund for voluntary sector housing for people with special needs. Details should be checked on government websites (see appendix 6).

■ Funding – Home Office

There are various sources of official funds for refugee-related projects. Here are only brief descriptions as circumstances change (latest information can be found at www.governmentfunding.org.uk or in the refugee integration section of the IND website – see appendix 6).

- *European Refugee Fund*. This fund, administered by the Home Office, is aimed at projects which receive refugees, encourage integration or facilitate return to home countries. Funding is normally provided for 50 per cent of costs, within a range of £30-80,000, for 12 months. The Home Office has consulted on the next phase of the fund, from 2005-10, in which it intends to prioritise voluntary return projects, although still with some funding for integration projects.

- *The Challenge Fund*. An annual fund aimed at pump-priming of projects assisting refugee integration, of between £20-50,000 over 12 months. The fund covers 100 per cent of costs, but applicants are expected to seek separate longer-term funding.

- *Purposeful Activities Fund*. Aimed at projects working with asylum seekers, this annual fund covers 100 per cent of costs for up to 12 months, with a normal limit of £40,000. Eligible projects are those that promote volunteering, form links with host communities or develop asylum seekers' skills.

- *Refugee Community Development Fund*. This small-scale grant fund (normal limit £5,000, exceptionally £10,000) is aimed at start-up, capacity building and similar costs for grassroots or community organisations, or those for whom refugees are a new target group. There is a 'call' for applications each year (currently, August-October).

- *Sunrise Programme*. This new programme is at pilot stage but will later be rolled-out nationally. The pilots (in Manchester, Leeds, Sheffield, London and Glasgow) will provide refugees with intensive, one-to-one support during the 28-day period following a positive decision, based on a 'personal integration plan' agreed with the caseworker.

- *Refugee Integration Loans.* Proposals for interest-free loans to individual newly-recognised refugees for items such as vocational training or deposits for rented accommodation, are due to take effect during 2005.

■ Funding – other sources

A wide range of grant-awarding bodies and foundations fund projects relating to new migrants, several of them mentioned in the examples in this guide. They are too numerous and details change too frequently to list them here. However, the website www.refugeeaccess.info publishes a monthly bulletin of information on currently-available funds, their criteria, and their deadlines.

Many interesting projects in the field of community integration are being funded by hact (www.hact.org.uk) and although there are no new 'calls' for potential funding their website is a useful reference point. The current Accommodate projects operate in five different areas and bring together RCOs, local authorities and housing providers to improve housing services and refugee integration.

❑ Staff skills

Staff skills are a key resource, not least because many important skills are scarce. This guide cannot cover this issue in depth, and there is information elsewhere on the tasks of recruiting, training and keeping staff – below is some limited guidance on skills and training needs for key groups of staff.

■ Support staff

The particular skills and knowledge likely to be needed include:

- language skills and/or skill in using interpreters
- skills in supporting vulnerable people in culturally-sensitive ways
- advice/welfare benefits skills and knowledge
- similar background knowledge to housing staff generally (see below).

Language skills

As seen in examples in chapters 4 and 5, organisations have dealt with these in different ways. Many have successfully recruited from the refugee community, others use established interpreter services or have established their own services (often in partnership with others). In practice, a combination of the two is likely to be needed. Where outside services are used, staff need training in how to make best use of them, and guidelines are needed on when or if other family members or friends may be used to interpret (see box).

Outline guidance on use of interpreters
(to be developed in detail to reflect local circumstances)

- identify language needs as soon as possible and provide an interpreter whenever needed
- make use of language skills within the staff team (identify who has validated skills, and establish rules on their availability)
- make use of approved interpreter services (identify them with conditions as to use and any charging arrangements)
- decide whether one-to-one, telephone or written service is required
- make appropriate appointment arrangements (eg book a one hour slot for personal interviews; arrange telephone interpretation if the client fails to make the appointment)
- decide on circumstances in which family or friends might be used (normally, as a last resort or in an emergency, and never on sensitive issues such as health care)
- agree not to use children as interpreters because of the likely sensitivity of the subject matter
- ensure that if a client is referred to another organisation it is made aware of their language needs.

Culturally-sensitive support skills

Chapter 5 dealt with support needs and the role of support workers; chapter 4 noted some of the sensitivities in dealing with new migrants as clients. In part, the skills needed are the same as for other support/resettlement services – but with the added dimensions of the culturally-varied nature of the client group, and their vulnerability as new migrants. Experienced providers such as Refugee HA deal with this in part by recruiting from the refugee community, in part by training and retaining staff to build up experience.

Refugee HA's approach to training support staff

RHA has a rolling training programme covering all core areas for every staff member providing support services. Under Supporting People the training programme covers: needs support and risk assessment, protection from abuse, service user involvement, mental health awareness, customer feedback.

In addition there are various induction or corporate training programmes on issues such as health and safety.

There is an appraisal system to identify staff training which is done annually, and weekly one:one supervision meetings from which training needs can be further identified.

RHA consults staff and managers on courses attended with regards to the delivery of the course, and its relevance and effectiveness in relation to the support work.

Advice/welfare benefits skills/knowledge
Skills needed are similar to those for clients in general, with two important provisos:

- housing and benefit entitlements depend on immigration status – appendix 3 gives details
- there are restrictions on the advice that can be given on immigration issues – see page 60.

■ Senior staff

Senior staff are likely to need skills in:

- project management and partnership working
- community development skills, including conflict resolution.

There is now an established body of practical guidance in both these areas (see chapter 7 and references in appendix 1).

■ Staff generally

All staff need knowledge and understanding of:

- different cultures and ethnic groups
- why and how people come to the UK.

Most organisations have training on BME issues and dealing with BME customers. This may, however, need adapting to reflect the needs of new migrants. The aims should be that:

- new migrant customers receive the same quality of service as any other customer
- staff are as aware of their needs and culture as they would be of long-established BME people in the area
- staff with regular contact with people for whom English is a second language are trained in clear communication (eg avoiding slang) that will help avoid misunderstanding
- no adverse image of asylum seekers or any other new migrant group is given, or reinforced.

As an example of the last point, it should be as unacceptable for a staff member to make a comment such as 'we don't have enough houses to allocate because there are so many asylum seekers' as it would be to make a similar comment relating to black people.

Issues that might be covered in general awareness training

- new migrant groups in the area, where they come from, languages spoken and cultural differences
- circumstances that lead people to leave their home countries and difficulties they have in reaching a safe country
- the organisation's own policies, including any commitments at cabinet/board level
- national policy on asylum and refugees (see chapters 2 and 3)
- rules relating to asylum seekers (limited help available, not able to work, etc – see chapter 3)
- entitlements of people with different immigration status (see appendix 3)
- the need for sensitivity on the part of staff (see chapter 4)
- the way that new migrants are covered by the organisation's rules about discrimination and equal treatment
- how staff should respond to comments from or hostility by other members of the public.

Local RCOs may be willing to help raise staff awareness by taking part in training sessions.

❑ Information resources

The table on the next page sets out some of the information needs that organisations may have, with references to other parts of this guide or to other sources where the information may be found. Website or other contact details are given in appendix 6.

Checklist on resources

- ✓ are you making the best use of the resource represented by people from new migrant communities in your area?
- ✓ have you explored the possibilities for mainstream funding of services for new migrants?
- ✓ what options are there for funding newly-established projects?
- ✓ are there any locally-available funds not mentioned here?
- ✓ have you considered what staff resources are already available in your organisation that might be used in this area?
- ✓ what extra skills do you need?
- ✓ are all staff aware of language needs and how to deal with them?
- ✓ have you checked to see what messages frontline staff are giving about asylum seekers, refugees, and their impact on availability of housing and other services?
- ✓ what steps do you need to take to get fully informed on these issues and have information available for key staff?

Information need	Possible source
Statistics on asylum/refugees and new migrants at national level	Home Office ICAR navigation guides
Statistics at local level	See commentary in chapters 3 and 9
Characteristics of new migrant groups (culture, language, religion, etc)	Information is scattered: • ICAR has navigation guides on some communities • JRF has published studies of young people from some ethnic groups • The Housing Corporation's study of Somali experiences is on their website • The Council for Homeless Northern Ireland's bulletin *Chainmail*, issue 3, has information on the range of communities in the province Seeking information from local groups themselves is also a useful approach
Descriptions of new migrant experiences and reasons for coming to the UK	The Guardian *Welcome to Britain* report; *Refugee voices* section of Refugee Action website; information from local groups; Moorehead, C (2005) – see appendix 7
Skill levels and economic contribution of new migrants	ASSET UK produces a newsletter and information on its website; the *2005 World Migration Report* by the International Organisation for Migration; RETAS website
Immigration rules and commentary on current developments	ICAR navigation guides; Joint Council for the Welfare of Immigrants website
Rules on assistance for asylum seekers and commentary on current developments	ICAR navigation guides NASS policy bulletins Asylum policy email service
Rules on housing/benefits for people of different immigration status	See appendix 3; see Shelter's Homelessness Act website for ongoing developments →

Information need	Possible source
Guidance on needs within new migrant groups (eg women, older people, children, disabled, etc)	See sources in chapter 5; Refugee Action has an information pack for women refugees covering a range of topics.
Advice on employment rights for migrant workers	leaflets in various languages available from DTI website
Guidance on working with asylum seekers as volunteers	ASSET UK website
Information for and about RCOs	Refugee Council – website has section devoted to RCOs; hact
Sources of funding for services/projects	See earlier in this chapter
News on political developments, policy and legal changes, media stories, campaigns	Asylum policy email service; Refugee Council newsletter; The Guardian *Society* website and email service

CHAPTER 9

DEVELOPING A REFUGEE HOUSING STRATEGY

What this chapter is about

- why a strategy is needed
- how to go about developing it
- what it should contain
- making sure it can be implemented
- links with other strategies
- monitoring and evaluation

So far this guide has looked at housing and support issues at the detailed level without looking at how they might form part of an overall strategy. This chapter is about how such a strategy might be developed. Different approaches will be needed in different kinds of organisation. A large local authority may have a refugee housing strategy for its area, or it may have a wider refugee integration strategy of which housing issues are one aspect. It may have a business plan for asylum accommodation if it is part of a NASS contract. In contrast, a housing association may not have an area-based strategy but may have a strategy for housing and supporting asylum seekers or refugees as part of its wider business plan. In some organisations, strategy on new migrants will be included in a broader BME strategy.

The chapter aims to give general guidance about developing strategies that is relevant to housing organisations. It also points to the many linkages with other aspects of an organisation's strategic work – such as race equality, community cohesion, Supporting People and so on. A further set of linkages is with the strategies of other organisations – for example, those of regional consortia, or the BME action plans of bodies such as the Housing Corporation and the Welsh Assembly Government. The chapter cannot give detailed guidance on housing strategies or business planning, which is available elsewhere.

❏ Why have a strategy?

Some organisations will simply respond to new needs (eg homelessness among new migrant groups) with ad hoc plans for, say, a hostel or other form of accommodation. There is nothing wrong with this as a way of 'getting started' in this field, but as soon as issues become more complex, priorities have to be decided or alternative ways of meeting need considered, a strategic approach is vital.

This is not to say that it has to be complicated. The essence of a strategy is to 'stand back' from day-to-day demands and take a considered, longer-term view, based on evidence of need and consideration of the range of options for meeting it, against the availability of resources.

One important reason for developing a strategy is to be able to access resources to meet needs. This might be finance – bidding for funds (such as Supporting People) from an outside body, or competing for available funds within an organisation. It might be partnerships – persuading other bodies, often with different priorities, to work together to meet needs. Or it might be staffing – arguing for new staff or to train existing staff. Starting or developing housing services for new migrant groups is likely to involve all of these.

Developing a strategy means setting out clearly what you intend to do, how you will do it and what impact you expect to have – and all of these are important in a period where there is intense pressure to demonstrate efficiency, customer satisfaction and value-for-money. They are especially important in getting 'buy in' from other partners and stakeholders – they are more likely to engage if they have had an input to a strategy and share the 'vision' for what is to be achieved.

> *'A good strategy should guide managerial action, focus energy, attention and resources, and help all staff and partners to understand what is intended to happen, and why.'*
>
> Sue Goss and Bob Blackaby (1998) *Designing Local Housing Strategies: a good practice guide*, CIH and LGA.

❏ Developing a strategy

■ Getting the process right

Although a written document is likely to be an output of the process, the main aim is to initiate action that will solve housing and related problems. So getting the process right is vital. Some of the key requirements are:

- getting commitment from the right level – the local authority cabinet, the housing association board, or simply from chief officers and senior managers

- having an inclusive process that involves new migrant communities themselves, and appropriate staff and other agencies who have expertise or knowledge to contribute
- clearly analysing the problems and options for solving them, based on the best available information
- recognising the diversity of needs – both between different groups, and within groups the different needs of women, older people, disabled people, etc
- establishing good communication and follow-up so that staff and partner organisations know what action is needed and someone is making sure that things happen.

Chapter 7 considers how to involve refugee community organisations and the development of wider partnerships to deliver services. These are a crucial part of any strategic approach. Issues about resources are dealt with in chapter 8.

■ Setting the Framework

- *Scope.* Choices will need to be made as to whether the strategy covers all new migrants or (for example) concentrates mainly on refugees. Further choices will be needed on the extent of the services covered – accommodation (chapter 4), support (chapter 5) or wider community needs (chapter 6). Decisions will partly depend on the scope of other related strategies – for example, those on homelessness, wider support (including Supporting People strategies), race equality or BME housing strategies, and strategies for promoting community cohesion.

- *Type.* Broadly, strategies can either be wide-ranging, embracing different kinds of resources and partnerships that will be needed for their implementation; or they can be more narrowly-focused as 'business plans' for delivering a particular operation or bidding for particular funds. Clearly a wide-ranging strategy involving multiple agencies needs to be prepared from scratch in ways which 'bind in' those agencies, or it is unlikely to succeed.

- *Boundaries.* A strategy might relate to the whole area of a local authority or housing association, or it might be a regional-level strategy for a consortium of providers. In any event, it is likely to focus on particular geographical areas where needs are concentrated.

- *Aims.* The strategic aims should be achievable and, as far as possible, measurable, so that outcomes can be assessed and the effectiveness of the strategy judged. The aims will of course be partly determined by decisions on other aspects of the strategy's scope. The aims may well have to be reviewed as the strategy is developed in detail and then implemented.

Aims of a Refugee Integration Strategy

Sheffield's integration strategy aims to:

- encourage refugees to choose to remain in Sheffield and play a full and equal part in the life of the city

- promote the development of high quality services that are responsive to the needs of refugees

- help refugees develop their potential and contribute to the cultural and economic life of the city

- raise awareness of refugees as a positive resource for all sectors and people within the city, and to counter negative stereotyping and discrimination

- support the development of refugee community organisations

- ensure that the needs of refugees are included in the plans of local strategic planning and regeneration partnerships.

Source: Sheffield Refugee Forum/City Council (2005) *New Lives: Refugee Integration Strategy 2005-2008.*

■ Gathering information

Building up a picture of the circumstances, needs and views of new migrants is important if the strategy is to be based on proper evidence. Because of the diversity of needs, and the fact that some parts of the communities might be 'hard to reach', a number of different approaches may be needed to build up this picture. As made clear in chapters 2 and 3, little information is available at local level on numbers and make-up of new migrant groups. Simply because many may be 'recent arrivals' they may not feature in normal sources of information such as the census, or even in previous BME housing surveys. Also, the way ethnic groups are traditionally defined may be out-of-date or not reveal newly-arrived groups (eg Kurdish refugees, Portuguese migrant workers – not distinguishable in the definitions used in the UK Census 2001).

Approaches that might be adopted include:
- checking up-to-date sources of information, such as lettings records, for information on ethnicity and other details of people already housed

- seeking information from accommodation providers of numbers and characteristics of asylum seekers as they reach the point of decision

- asking RCOs and advice centres for information they may have gathered on housing needs

- consulting wider service providers (eg health) and interpreter services for evidence of needs, language groups, etc

- setting up focus groups or special surveys to look at particular needs where information is lacking.

In one London Borough, an RCO conducted a comprehensive survey of its community and was able to present the authority with detailed evidence of housing need. Focus groups have been used to identify needs within BME groups – for example, of younger people – that may not be revealed by more general surveys.

Some difficulties that may have to be faced are:

- language – making sure researchers have relevant language skills
- 'hidden needs' – for example, people staying with relatives and/or people whose immigration status is in question
- gender sensitivities – some women may prefer to be interviewed by a woman.

The points that were made in chapter 4 about the skills needed for interviewing people apply particularly in these cases, because the organisation (not the customer) is taking the initiative in asking the questions and has to gain the interviewee's confidence.

■ Identifying needs and how they can be met

By this stage those developing the strategy should have collected a lot of evidence from different sources, some more reliable or detailed than others, on different kinds of need. They should be categorised in ways which make the information more readily usable at the next stage, which is to develop detailed objectives and options for achieving them. For example, some needs might be met by administrative changes (eg in lettings policies) whereas others might be longer-term and need more resource input. Some problems might be directly solvable by the organisation whereas others might need wider collaboration. Almost inevitably, some needs will require more extensive investigation and addressing them fully might have to wait until this is complete, in which case some interim action might be appropriate.

It is unlikely that there are *no* existing programmes or policies relevant to new migrants, but they may not be meeting (or fully meeting) the needs. Such programmes and policies should if possible be brought within the remit of the new strategy and reconsidered as part of it.

■ Setting objectives and targets

More detailed *objectives* can now be set, which relate the overall aims decided earlier to the actual problems and issues identified. This then enables *indicators* to be established against which success can be judged. These might be based on national indicators – such as those in the government's policy document *Integration Matters*.

Indicators of integration based on those in *Integration Matters*

- employment and unemployment rates of refugees compared with those of the general population
- proportion of refugees demonstrating English-language fluency within two years of receiving refugee status
- number of refugees involved in voluntary work
- number of refugees, and their children, in touch with community organisations (including local groups and wider community life)
- proportion of refugees taking up British citizenship once they are qualified to do so
- proportion of refugees reporting racial, cultural or religious harassment
- reported satisfaction of refugees with their housing, compared with the general population
- educational success of children from refugee families

However, it is important that achievement against indicators is measurable, and that information is available to assess progress. This is a weakness of some of the official indicators which needs to be taken into account in developing local ones. Also, indicators should reflect local priorities. There is no point in using an indicator if there is no local programme intended to address it. There is LGA advice on developing local indicators of community cohesion which may usefully be adapted for refugee strategies.

Choice of indicators allows *targets* to be set – which might be expressed as *outputs* (eg production of a local 'myth busting' leaflet) or *outcomes* (eg raise housing satisfaction levels among refugees to the same level as those for long-term residents, within five years).

◼ Choosing options and creating an action plan

The core of the strategy is the set of actions which will actually be taken. Deciding on these requires options to be considered and appraised. For example, if more emergency accommodation is needed for new migrants, is there an existing service which could be adapted or is a new one required? – if so, is there a potential partner who already has experience of this kind of service?

Most of this guide is aimed at helping housing organisations consider and choose options for improved services to new migrants – whether they provide them themselves, or do so in partnership with others. Consultation with potential partners, and with refugee and other community organisations, is most important. CIH also publishes detailed guidance on option appraisal if this is needed.

The *action plan* is a series of detailed steps intended to lead to specific service developments. It might take the following form:

- identifying the *issue* (eg new migrants being concentrated in certain areas with poor housing conditions)
- establish an *indicator* (eg percentage of new migrants housed in different areas) and planned *outcomes* (eg number of neighbourhoods where new migrants are housed to be increased within three years)
- decide on *action* (eg resettlement support for new migrants electing to move to new areas)
- say how it will be *implemented* (eg recruit extra support staff with relevant language skills), over what *timescale*, with what resources and who is responsible for it.

The strategy and action plans may well be published in draft as a means of consulting partners and refugee groups, and obtaining their comments to inform the final version.

Plans may be contingent on securing finance – for example through bidding processes – and may need to be revised if bids fail. It is therefore useful to distinguish between resources that are within an agency's own discretion and those that depend on decisions elsewhere.

❑ Relationship to other strategies

One reason for having (say) a refugee housing strategy may be as a way of focussing attention on and getting commitment to a neglected issue. But that does not mean that the strategy stands alone – it has to fit in with or relate to other strategies. For example, there is likely to be a wider housing strategy, including a homelessness strategy, which should reflect refugee and other needs. There may already be a separate BME housing strategy, a strategy to promote community cohesion or a statutory Race Equality Scheme. There will be a Supporting People strategy on which new migrant support services may depend for funding.

A *business plan* for an asylum team or refugee support service will need to fit within the wider business plan for the organisation – whether a local authority or housing association – and show how it will contribute to it or draw resources from it.

At local authority level, there will be wider community strategies and local strategic partnerships (community planning partnerships in Scotland), probably involving many of the same agencies (such as health and police) who need to 'buy in' to the refugee housing strategy. These may have led to neighbourhood renewal strategies in particular areas or to special programmes like Housing Market Renewal Pathfinders – which should include new migrant needs if they are relevant. Authorities carrying out option appraisals or considering transfer plans for their own housing stock should consider whether refugee groups should be consulted or involved (see guidance in Mullins, D *et al*, 2004). Many authorities also have an economic development strategy and this should cover employment prospects for refugees.

At regional level, many regions have consortia dealing with asylum seeker accommodation which have broadened their work to develop wider refugee integration strategies. Every English region now has a Regional Housing Strategy which should reflect new migrant housing needs. In the West Midlands, the Centre for Urban and Regional Studies (CURS) at Birmingham University has been commissioned to analyse the regional housing market, to inform the regional strategy. This analysis has included an assessment of numbers and distribution of asylum seekers and refugees in the region and of their impact on the housing market. CURS also made recommendations for the strategy (see www.curs. bham.ac.uk/wmrhr/).

The Scottish Refugee Intergation Forum (2005) has, and the Welsh Assembly Government is developing, a strategy for refugee integration.

❑ Monitoring and evaluation

It is important to consider early on how the strategy will be monitored and success judged – 'how do we know whether the strategy is a success?' Apart from formally considering data that show whether outputs or outcomes have been achieved in the timescale set, there is clearly an important role for RCOs and other community groups to provide feedback and contribute to future reviews of the strategy. Offical guidance on ethnic monitoring may be usefully adapted for use with refugee strategies.

Checklist on developing a strategy

✓ does your organisation have a strategy for new migrant housing and support needs?

✓ if it does, should it be reviewed?

✓ if it doesn't, is a strategy needed, and if so what kind of strategy should it be?

✓ are there other strategies that already exist – in your organisation or in other agencies – that it should reflect?

✓ how will you go about getting commitment to the strategy within your organisation and from other agencies?

✓ how will you involve new migrant groups and make sure they 'own' the strategy?

✓ how will you know whether the strategy is successful?

And a final checklist …

Final checklist

✓ Have you found this guide useful?

✓ Do you have any suggestions for improvements in any future edition?

✓ Has it helped you to take action on these issues in your organisation or local area?

✓ Have you sought information from or visited any of the practical examples mentioned? – was this helpful?

✓ Have you changed your policy or initiated a new project, as a result of the guide? – if so, please let us know.

✓ Have you thought about publicising your project, for example by entering it for the National Housing Awards?

Comments and suggestions are welcome. Please send them to the author at john.perry@cih.org or to policy@cih.org – or write to CIH at the address at the front of the guide.

Appendix 1

References and Sources used in the Text

References below relate to the page numbers quoted. Appendix 7 gives a list of key reports and publications for those wanting to review the current literature. Where a source is included in appendix 7, only the author, date, and page or chapter references are given here.

■ Chapter 2

page 5: **Home Office research report...** Carey-Wood, J (1997), p27.

page 5: **Chief Executive of the Housing Corporation...** HC Press Release No. 22/04, Friday 25 June 2004. *Chief Executive pledges Corporation support for refugees.*

page 5: **National organisations such as CIH and NHF...** see CIH (2003), and the NHF paper *Housing and support options for refugee and asylum seekers* available at www.housing.org.uk (July 2004).

page 7: **Migration, asylum seekers and refugees – some basic facts...** information from official sources, available at www.statistics.gov.uk and in the quarterly asylum statistics (available at www.homeoffice.gov.uk/rds/immigration1.html).

page 7: **Probably numbering several thousands...** a recent report by the NAO (2005) *Returning failed asylum applicants* puts the number of asylum seekers whose claims have been refused and are still in the UK at between 155,000 and 283,500.

page 8: **A recent assessment...** figure for total number of asylum seekers in London taken from Mayor of London (2005) *Into the Labyrinth: Legal advice for asylum seekers in London*, p25.

■ Chapter 3

page 10: **Who are they?...** all statistics in this section come from the Home Office quarterly asylum statistics, except for those (including the pie chart) in the sub-section **And other new migrants?** which come from the Home Office (2005) *Control of Immigration: Statistics UK 2004.*

page 12: **The Needs of Newcomers...** this is based partly on the description of support networks in Glasgow in Wren, K (2004), chapter 3.

page 13: **Never assume...** quote by Dash Koci from personal correspondence with the author, with permission.

page 13: **Although many asylum seekers speak English most do not...** see DWP (2002) *Refugees' Opportunities and Barriers in Employment and Training.*

page 15: **Entering Britain as an asylum seeker...** this and the following section are largely based on the ICAR Navigation Guide *Key Issues: UK asylum law and process* (ICAR, 2004).

page 15: **The guide does not cover the issue of people held in detention centres...** at the end of 2004 there were 1,515 people in detention who had previously sought asylum – see Home Office (2005) *Asylum Statistics UK 2004*. Amnesty International says 25,000 may have been detained in total in 2004. See Amnesty International (2005) *Seeking Asylum is not a Crime – detention of people who have sought asylum.*

page 19: **Resettlement is the organised movement...** based on the ICAR Navigation Guide *Resettlement Programmes and the UK* (ICAR, 2004).

■ **Chapter 4**

page 21: **'As a result of refugee's fears of hostility...'** quote from Carey-Wood, J (1997), p25.

page 22: **Possible symptoms of this stress have been identified as...** Carey-Wood, J (1997), p23.

page 22: **Experienced workers in this field point out...** based on discussion with Joan MacFarlane of the Sheffield Asylum Health Team (see chapter 5).

page 24: **Numbers can be substantial...** figures on emergency accommodation and induction centres in this and the following paragraph are from National Audit Office (2005), pp 12-14.

page 26: **Accommodation and support for asylum seekers (box)** Adapted from Whiting, C (2004) *Housing and Supporting Asylum Seekers and Refugees*. People for Action, p7.

page 26: **In the past, there have been doubts about the quality...** dealt with in NAO (2005), pp 26-27.

page 27: **NASS has resolved many of the problems of placing people...** for continuing evidence of difficulties, see NAO (2005), p16.

page 27: **Some 18,000 people are housed under the scheme in London...** statistics from London Asylum Seekers Consortium, end of 2004.

page 27: **The 28 day period... (box)** Examples of the period being effectively much shorter are given in hact (2003), p32.

page 28: **Evidence from Glasgow...** based on Wren, K (2004), chapter 5.

page 28: **Communities Scotland has developed a guide...** for further information contact the HomePoint team (homepoint@communitiesscotland.gov.uk).

page 30: **Save the Children publishes a guide...** obtainable by email (contact K.Kenny@savethechildren.org.uk).

page 30: **Glasgow's Family Reunion project...** for further information see the Home Office website (www.ind.homeoffice.gov.uk/ind/en/home/laws___policy/refugee_integration0/funding/challenge_fund/list_of_projects_s.html).

page 32: **However, it is both government policy...** see ODPM (2005) *Sustainable Communities: settled homes; changing lives – a strategy for tackling homelessness* (available at www.odpm.gov.uk/stellent/groups/odpm_homelessness/documents/page/odpm_home_035965.pdf).

page 32: **In England the code of guidance...** ODPM (2002) *Homelessness Code of Guidance*, para 8.33.

page 32: **In Wales the guidance...** Welsh Assembly Government (2003) *Code of Guidance for Local Authorities on Allocation of Accommodation and Homelessness*, para 14.22.

page 32: **Both the English and the Welsh guidance...** see above, paras 8.30 and 14.18 respectively.

page 34: **Health workers dealing with new migrants...** discussion with Joan MacFarlane of the Sheffield Asylum Health Team (see chapter 5).

page 34: **A guide to refugee-related schemes is published by hact...** hact (2002) *A Foot in the Door – Rent Deposit Schemes* (see www.hact.org.uk).

page 34: **The Chartered Institute of Environmental Health publishes standards...** see www.cieh.org/about/policy/advisory/ho2k002.htm (NB these are being updated).

page 36: **Possible reasons for destitution...** based on the reports by Woodcock, B (2004) *Destitution and asylum seekers: a human rights issue*, Coventry Refugee Centre and Refugee Action; and Leicester Refugee and Asylum Seekers' Voluntary Sector Forum (2005) *A Report on Destitution in the Asylum System in Leicester*.

page 36: **A study of 38 destitute asylum seekers in Coventry...** see above.

■ Chapter 5

page 47: **Refugees and other new migrants are very diverse in their needs...** this paragraph is based on a note from Ann Branson, Leicester City Council, 2004.

page 47: **Objectives of a support service...** list based partly on an internal document supplied by RHA.

page 56: **Example of benefit-related problems...** from the Birmingham Refugee Resource Centre annual report 2003/04.

page 57: **In Glasgow... some schools have bi-lingual units...** from Wren, K (2004), chapter 3.

page 57: **However, there are a number of potential obstacles...** based partly on BMA (2004) *Asylum Seekers and their Health* and partly on discussion with Joan MacFarlane of the Sheffield Asylum Health Team.

page 58: **Housing is the key to stabilising a person's mental health...** quote from discussion with author.

page 60: **complaints about the quality of legal advice services...** see for example Mayor of London (2005) *Into the Labyrinth: Legal advice for asylum seekers in London*, p54.

page 60: **Advice is available from a range of sources, such as...** based on Mayor of London (2005), see above, p39.

page 60: **In Northern Ireland, the Law Centre...** based on correspondence with Fidelma O'Hagan of the Law Centre.

page 60: **It has been a culture shock...** The quote is from a 25 year old who came to Britain in 2000 and has now been accepted as a refugee.

page 60: **Only 17 per cent of new arrivals speak English well...** from the major survey by DWP (2002) *Refugees' Opportunities and Barriers in Employment and Training*.

page 61: **Home Office research shows that there is a shortage of classes ...** see Home Office (2004) *English Language Training for Refugees in London and the Regions*.

page 61: **Research by the National Institute of Adult Continuing Education has shown...** quoted from the NIACE website (see: www.asset-uk.org.uk/niace.htm).

page 61: **Women refugees may be deterred from joining mixed training groups...** see ICAR (2004) *Women refugees and asylum seekers in the UK – Navigation Guide*.

page 61: **Home Office-sponsored research also argues...** from Carey-Wood, J (1997), p40.

page 62: **there are an estimated 1,000 refugee doctors who could work in the NHS...** reported in The Guardian, 25 November 2004.

page 64: **Good practice lessons included...** based on some of the lessons set out in the evaluation report, see: Riseborough, M (2004) *Creating Better Services – CDS floating support service for people with leave to remain status*. CDS, Liverpool.

■ **Chapter 6**

page 73: **But there are also government policies about 'integration' and 'community cohesion'...** see the appropriate websites – refugee integration (www.ind.homeoffice.gov.uk/ind/en/home/laws___policy/refugee_ integration0.html?); community cohesion (www.communitycohesion.gov.uk).

page 73: **The Home Office's (2005) strategy defines integration as...** Home Office (2005), p5.

page 73: **There are also separate CIH guidance and case studies...** see Blackaby, B (2004) and Robinson, D *et al* (2004).

page 74: **Refugees interviewed in the Glasgow/London study...** see Agar and Strang (2004).

page 76: **In the Henley Green area of Coventry...** based on material supplied by ICAR and Coventry Refugee Centre.

page 77: **In Glasgow, for example, there are ten local networks...** see Wren, K (2004), chapter 3.

page 78: **In adapting these to the circumstances of new migrant groups, they need to...** this section is based substantially on Blackaby, B (2004), pp 62-64.

page 78: **There is guidance available from CIH...** for example, CIH (2003) *Equality and Diversity*. Good Practice Briefing No 26. CIH.

page 78: **Among other issues, local policies and practices should...** based partly on the CRE draft code (CRE, 2005).

page 79: **Refugee Action is running a refugee awareness project...** see their website (www.refugee-action.org.uk/ourwork/projects.aspx).

page 80: **The Yorkshire and Humberside Consortium has a media strategy...** information from John Donegan at the Consortium.

page 82: **Local residents provide practical help for newcomers...** Gladys Chilton's name is used with permission.

■ Chapter 7

page 88: **Working with refugee community organsiations...** This section is partly based on work carried out for the guide by hact and partly on a structured discussion with a number of RCOs and RCHAs in May, 2005. It also draws on the report by hact (2002) *The Role of RCOs and RCHAs in Providing Housing for Refugees and Asylum Seekers in London.*

page 90: **For example, the Scottish Refugee Council has tests...** discussion with Peter Barry of the SRC. For information on *Framework for Dialogue* see the SRC website (www.scottishrefugeecouncil.org.uk).

page 90: **Such RCOs:...** points taken from the above source.

page 93: **Stock transfer has led...** see Mullins, D *et al* (2004).

page 96: **Its affordable housing programme...** see Housing Corporation (2005) *The National Affordable Housing Programme 2006-08: Prospectus* (available at www.housingcorp.gov.uk).

■ Chapter 8

page 99: **It is a complex topic and detailed guidance is available elsewhere...** see for example Garnett, D and Perry , J (2005) *Housing Finance.* CIH.

page 102: **there is information elsewhere on the tasks of recruiting, training and keeping staff...** see Green, H (2004) *Staff Recruitment and Retention: A good practice guide.* CIH.

■ Chapter 9

page 108: **The chapter cannot give detailed guidance...** see for example the ODPM website www.odpm.gov.uk and its section on Effective Housing Strategies and Plans.

page 109: **Developing a Strategy...** this section draws heavily from chapter 2 of Blackaby, B and Chahal, K (2000) *Black and Minority Ethnic Housing Strategies; a good practice guide.* CIH, FBHO and the Housing Corporation.

page 112: **Focus groups have been used...** examples are given in Ratcliffe, P *et al* (2001) *Breaking Down the Barriers – Improving Asian access to social rented housing.* CIH (for Bradford CC, FBHO and the Housing Corporation).

page 113: **Indicators of integration...** quoted in Sheffield Refugee Forum/City Council (2005) *New Lives: Refugee Integration Strategy 2005-2008.*

page 113: **There is LGA advice...** see LGA and others (2004).

page 113: **CIH also publishes detailed guidance on option appraisal...** see Goss, S and Blackaby, B (1998) *Designing Local Housing Strategies: a good practice guide.* CIH and LGA.

page 115: **Official guidance on ethnic monitoring...** see NRU (2004) *Ethnic Monitoring: Benefit* and *Ethnic Monitoring: Involvement* (both available at www.neighbourhood.gov.uk).

APPENDIX 2

GUIDANCE ON THE LEGAL POSITION FOR HOUSING PROVIDERS INTERVIEWING NEW MIGRANTS

New migrants may have difficulty dealing with housing providers because of fears that information they provide may not be treated in confidence. The position is different for local authorities and housing associations, and this appendix gives recommended guidance for each.

■ Housing associations

Because HAs are not part of government they neither have to supply information to the immigration authorities, nor can they obtain it from them. Applicants who are new migrants should therefore be treated in the same way as any other applicant as regards the confidentially of any interview. If it appears that an applicant may not be eligible for housing benefit (see appendix 3), the association may well ask for proof of ability to pay the rent (as they may do for any applicant).

■ Local authorities

Local authorities are in a different position because they are part of government. They should ensure that they can provide clear information about confidentiality policies and the limits of them. This should include a statement that:

- Advice services are offered in confidence and clear information will be provided about whether any applications for housing or other help will be notified to the Home Office.
- Advice services can be offered to people who do not give their name or address, but this may limit the advice available.
- The authority does not routinely share information with the Home Office, but may contact them or respond to requests in certain situations:
  - If the Home Office contact the local authority with a written request for information about a specific person whom they suspect of committing an immigration offence, the local authority has to provide the Home Office with the information they may have about where that person is or was living.
  - The local authority (as with all citizens and residents) has a general duty to assist the police in any criminal enquiries.
  - If an application for local authority housing or homelessness services is made, the local authority has to establish whether the applicant is eligible

and may contact the Home Office for information about this. Contact will not be made with the Home Office before the applicant is informed, and will not be made if the applicant withdraws their application at this stage.

- If an applicant is placed in accommodation under a contract with NASS (the National Asylum Support Service), then the Home Office will be informed of this.
- If an application for accommodation or support is made to social services by someone who is an asylum seeker whose application has been rejected, or is someone who has entered the country illegally or has overstayed the period in which they were granted permission to be here, then if social services know this they must inform the Home Office.

• If the applicant does not have proof of their eligibility for accommodation, and asks the authority to contact the Home Office, then it will do so.

Appendix 3

Legal Provisions on Help under Homelessness Legislation, Housing Benefit and Entitlement to Accommodation

Figure A3.1: UK Immigration Status and the Homelessness Duty – Eligibility of people of different status for help under homelessness legislation
Note: definitions of terms used in figures A3.1 – A3.3 are given in A3.4.

Status	Conditions of eligibility
British or Irish citizen	Entitled if • They apply for assistance in Scotland; or • They apply for assistance in England, Wales or Northern Ireland **AND** they are *habitually resident* in the *common travel area*.
Asylum seeker	Not entitled (a small number of persons who applied for asylum before 3 April 2000 who have not subsequently received a negative decision on their asylum claim may be entitled in certain circumstances).
Refugee	Entitled (together with their dependants) without further conditions.
Humanitarian protection Discretionary leave Exceptional leave	Entitled without further conditions but only if their leave is granted without the condition that there is no recourse to *public funds*.
Foreign nationals subject to immigration control (ie who are not in any of the classes above or below)	Entitled only if: a. they have been granted *indefinite leave* **AND** they are *habitually resident* in the *common travel area* **AND** are not the subject of an undertaking signed by sponsor to maintain them; or b. they are a *sponsored immigrant* subject to an undertaking and at least five years have passed since they entered the UK or the undertaking was made (whichever is the later); or c. they are a *sponsored immigrant* subject to an undertaking but all those who signed the undertaking have now died **AND** they are *habitually resident in the common travel area*; or ➔

Status (continued)	Conditions of eligibility (continued)
	d. they left the territory of Montserrat after 01/11/1995 due to the volcanic eruption; or e. they are in receipt of income support or income-based jobseekers allowance (other than for the reason of temporary disruption of funds).

EEA nationals* (who are not in any of the classes above or below)
 	
*including Swiss nationals
	Entitled if
	• They apply for assistance in Scotland; or
	• They apply for assistance in England, Wales or Northern Ireland and they are:
	  – Economically active (covered by the regulations for *workers*, the self employed, *former workers* and their family members
	  – Someone with another *right to reside* in the UK **AND** they are *habitually resident* in the *common travel area*; or
	  – a person who would qualify for an EU residence permit if they applied for one (for guidance see the Housing Benefit Guidance Manual, C7 Annex B, paragraphs 9-12) **AND** they are *habitually resident* in the *common travel area*.

EEA accession nationals (sometimes known as A8 nationals)	Entitled if:
	• they apply for assistance in Scotland; or
	• they apply for housing in England, Wales, or Northern Ireland **AND**
	  – have worked in the UK for an uninterrupted period of at least 12 months; or
	  – had indefinite leave to remain in the UK granted before 01/05/04; or
	  – are now self-employed in the UK; or
	  – are now working in the UK and on the *worker registration scheme* or have applied to go on to it within the first 30 days of starting their job; or
	  – have an EU residence permit in the UK or would qualify for one **AND** are *habitually resident* in the *common travel area*; or
	  – have some other right to reside in the UK **AND** are *habitually resident* in the *common travel area*.

ECSMA or CESC nationals	Entitled if they have been granted *leave* to be in the UK by the immigration authorities which has not expired; **AND** they are *habitually resident* in the *common travel area*.

References (statutory instruments and statutory rules):
England: SI 2000 No. 701 as amended by SI 2004 No. 1235.
Scotland: SI 2000 No. 706.
Wales: SI 2000 No. 1079.
Northern Ireland: SI 2000 No.706 and NI SR 2004 No. 199.

Figure A3.2: UK Immigration Status and Housing-related Benefits – Eligibility of people of different status for housing benefit and council tax benefit

Status	Conditions of eligibility
British or Irish citizen	Entitled if they are *habitually resident* in the *common travel area.*
Asylum seeker	As figure A3.1.
Refugee	As figure A3.1.
Humanitarian Protection Discretionary Leave Exceptional Leave	As figure A3.1.
Foreign nationals subject to immigration control (ie who are not in any of the classes above or below)	Entitled if: • they satisfy any of the conditions (a) to (d) in figure A3.1; or • they have *limited leave* but their funds from abroad are temporarily disrupted and there is a reasonable expectation they will resume within 3 months. They are entitled to HB/CTB for up to 42 days in any one period of *leave.*
EEA nationals* (who are not in any of the classes above or below) *including Swiss nationals	Entitled if: • they satisfy any of the conditions in figure A3.1 which relate to a person who applies for housing assistance in England (whether or not they are claiming HB in England or elsewhere in the UK); or • they were entitled to either income support, income-based jobseeker's allowance or the state pension credit or housing benefit or council tax benefit on 30/04/2004 and have remained entitled to at least one of those benefits since.
EEA accession nationals (sometimes known as A8 nationals)	Entitled if: • they satisfy any of the conditions in figure A3.1 which relate to a person who applies for housing assistance in England (whether or not they are claiming HB in England or elsewhere in the UK); or • they were entitled to either income support, income-based jobseeker's allowance or the state pension credit or housing benefit or council tax benefit on the 30/04/2004 and have remained entitled to at least one of those benefits since.
ECSMA or CESC nationals	As figure A3.1.

References (statutory instruments and statutory rules):
England, Scotland and Wales: SI 2000 No. 636 and Regulation 7A of the Housing Benefit (General) Regulations 1987 as variously amended including amendments by Regulation 6 of SI 2004 No. 1232. Northern Ireland: SI 2000 No.71 and Regulation 7A of the Housing Benefit (General) (Northern Ireland) Regulations 1987 as variously amended including amendments by Regulation 6 of NI SR 2004 No. 197.

Figure A3.3: UK Immigration Status and Social Housing – Eligibility of people of different status for letting of LA or HA accommodation

A person will be allocated housing if they:
- are selected to be a secure, Scottish secure or introductory tenant of a local authority or NIHE; local authority secure or introductory tenant or;
- in England and Wales are nominated by the local authority to be an assured tenant (including assured shorthold) of a registered social landlord (whether under a voluntary arrangement or otherwise); or
- are selected for transfer (but not exchange) of a local authority or NIHE tenancy.

Status	Conditions of eligibility
British or Irish citizen	As figure A3.1.
Asylum seeker	Not entitled.
Refugee	As figure A3.1.
Humanitarian Protection Discretionary Leave Exceptional Leave	As figure A3.1.
Foreign nationals subject to immigration control (ie who are not in any of the classes above or below)	Entitled if they satisfy any of the conditions (a) to (d) in figure A3.1.
EEA nationals* (who are not in any of the classes above or below) *including Swiss nationals	Entitled if: • they apply for housing in Scotland; or • they apply for housing in England, Wales or Northern Ireland **AND** they satisfy any of the conditions in figure A3.1 which relates to an *EEA national* who applies for housing assistance in England (whether or not they are applying for housing in England, Wales or Northern Ireland).
EEA accession nationals (sometimes known as A8 nationals)	Entitled if: • they apply for housing in Scotland; • they apply for housing in Wales **AND** they satisfy any of the conditions in figure A3.1 which relates to an *EEA national* (not *EEA accession national*) who applies for housing assistance in Wales; or • they apply for housing in England or Northern Ireland **AND** they satisfy any of the conditions in figure A3.1 which relates to an *EEA accession national* who applies for housing assistance in England (whether or not they are applying for housing in England, or Northern Ireland).
ECSMA or CESC nationals	As figure A3.1.

References (statutory instruments and statutory rules):
England: SI 2000 No. 706 and SI 2002 No. 3264 as amended by SI 2004 No. 1235.
Scotland: SI 2000 No. 706.
Wales: SI 2003 No. 239.
Northern Ireland: SI 2000 No.706 and NI SR 2004 No. 198.

Figure A3.4: Definition of terms used in previous figures

Term	Description
Asylum seeker	A person who has made an application for asylum as a refugee due to fear of persecution in their country of origin, which has not yet been finally decided.
Common travel area	The UK, the Republic of Ireland, the Channel Islands and the Isle of Man.
Discretionary leave	A form of leave granted at discretion of the Home Secretary. It is granted to asylum seeker's whose claim for asylum has been refused where the applicant does not meet the criteria for *humanitarian protection* but there are other exceptional circumstances why they should be allowed to stay in the UK.
ECSMA or CESC nationals	Nationals of a state that has ratified either the European Convention on Social and Medical Assistance or the Council of Europe Social Charter. As at 1 May 2005 all of the *EEA* and *EEA accession states* (with the exception of Liechtenstein, Lithuania and Slovenia) have also ratified ECSMA or CESC. For an up to date list of countries that have ratified the ECSMA or CESC follow: http://conventions.coe.int/Treaty/Commun/ListeTraites.asp?CM=8&CL=ENG (see treaties 14 and 35). As at 1 May 2005 the only states other than the EEA states that have ratified either of the treaties are Croatia, Macedonia and Turkey.
EEA nationals	Nationals of the following states: Austria, Belgium, Cyprus, Denmark, Finland, France, Germany, Greece, Iceland, Italy, Liechtenstein, Luxembourg, Malta, Netherlands, Norway, Portugal, Spain, Sweden, Switzerland.* * Note: strictly speaking Switzerland is not part of the EEA but Swiss nationals are treated as EEA nationals by a separate treaty with the EEA and by UK regulations (SI 2002 No. 1241). The UK and Ireland are of course member states of the EEA but for ease of reference are dealt with separately in these figures. Cyprus and Malta joined the EU with the other accession states in May 2004 but with full rights immediately on accession. →

Term (continued)	Description (continued)
EEA accession nationals	Nationals of the following states: Czech Republic, Estonia, Hungary, Latvia, Lithuania, Poland, Slovakia, Slovenia (for Cyprus and Malta see EEA nationals). From 1 May 2004 nationals of these states will only qualify for benefits and housing assistance if they are working and are registered under the *worker registration scheme*; or have some other *right to reside* in the UK and they are *habitually resident* in the *common travel area*. Those who were granted *indefinite leave* before 1 May 2004 or who have completed an uninterrupted 12 month period of legal work in the UK also qualify.
Exceptional leave	Exceptional leave is a form of leave granted at the discretion of the Home Secretary. It is granted to people when it is considered that they should be allowed to remain in the UK on humanitarian grounds. Since 1 April 2003 it has only been granted to people who have not made an application for asylum (ie an asylum seeker). Applicants for asylum whose application is refused may instead be granted *discretionary leave* or *humanitarian protection*.

Former worker	A person who is:*
	• retired after working the UK for at least 12 months prior to reaching age 65 (60 for a woman); or
	• incapable of work through sickness or industrial injury and who
	  – is entitled to incapacity benefit or industrial injuries benefit, or
	  – previously resided in the UK for two years or more, or
	  – has a spouse who is a British citizen; or
	• seeking reinstatement or re-employment with the same employer after being temporarily laid off; or
	• actively seeking work (for a period of up to six months).
	
	*Note: this is a very complex and rapidly developing area of law: the above only provides a broad summary.

Habitually resident	A person will be habitually resident if there is a degree of permanence about residence in the *common travel area*. Habitual residence is not defined but guidance based on case law (see Housing Benefit Guidance Manual, paragraph C7.175) suggests that the following factors are relevant: • length and continuity of residence; • future intentions; • employment prospects; • reasons for coming to the UK; and • centre of interest (ie the intention to follow a settled way of life in the UK and the ties they have formed). →

Term (continued)	Description (continued)
Habitually resident – continued	Any person (of any nationality) returning to the *common travel area* from abroad and re-establishing their ties will be habitually resident on their return.
Humanitarian protection	A form of *leave* granted at discretion of the Home Secretary. It is granted to asylum seekers whose claim for asylum has been refused but it is accepted that they would at be at risk of their life or of degrading treatment if they returned to their country of origin.
Immigration control	A person will be subject to immigration control if they require permission from the immigration authorities to enter or remain in the UK (including a person who has been granted *indefinite leave*). A person will be subject to immigration control if they are a national of a foreign state which is not an EEA16, A2 or A8 member state.
Illegal entrant	A person who enters the UK without *leave* who has not been granted *temporary admission*.
Indefinite leave (to remain)	A form of *leave* which is open ended (ie not time limited). A person with indefinite leave without any condition that they have no recourse to *public funds* is said to have *settled status*.
Leave	Legal permission to be in the UK granted by the immigration authorities under the immigration acts. Leave can be for a fixed period, known as *limited leave* or open ended – in which case it is known as *indefinite leave*. A person who requires leave but does not have it is known as an *illegal entrant*. A person whose period of leave has expired is known as an *overstayer*. Leave does not include *temporary admission* granted to a person on entry whilst their immigration status is determined by the authorities.
Limited leave	A form of *leave* which is for a fixed period.
Overstayer	A person whose *leave* has expired and has not been renewed and for whom no appeal is pending.
Public funds	A claim for any of the following benefits or assistance: • income support, income-based jobseeker's allowance, state pension credit, housing benefit or council tax benefit (and certain other benefits), or; • a full housing duty as a homelessness person.
Refugee	A person whose claim for asylum under the terms of the 1951 United Nations Convention has been accepted. Refugees are entitled to have their dependants settle with them. →

Term (continued)	Description (continued)
Right to reside (EEA nationals and EEA accession nationals only)	*Workers, former workers*, the self employed and work seekers (for a period of up to six months) have the right to reside in another member state (but for EEA accession nationals see also the *worker registration scheme*). However, under the EEA treaties certain other economically inactive persons also have the right to reside in the UK (such as students and retired persons who are not *former workers*) provided that they are self-sufficient and will not be an unreasonable burden on the member state (see Housing Benefit Guidance Manual part C7 for guidance of how the authorities are likely to apply this test). This is an exceptionally complex and developing area of the law and the above is only a broad summary.
Settled status	A person who is a national of a foreign state who has been granted *indefinite leave* to remain in the UK by the immigration authorities. Their passport will be endorsed as such and accompanied by an authenticating stamp issued by the Home Office Immigration and Nationality Directorate.
Sponsored immigrant	A person who has been granted *leave* to remain in the UK to join a family member here. In some cases an undertaking is required for this (a legally binding agreement to maintain and accommodate them).
Temporary admission	The period of grace allowed a person who has entered the UK but whose application for *leave* or for asylum has not yet been determined.
Worker (EEA nationals and Swiss nationals only)	Anyone engaged in paid employment for work which is 'effective and genuine'. This can include work which is low paid or part-time. The term worker does not include a UK citizen unless they have previously worked in another EEA state and are returning to the UK. It is possible for a *former worker* to be treated as a worker indefinitely on retirement.
Worker registration scheme (EEA accession nationals only)	*EEA accession nationals* who had not completed an uninterrupted period of 12 months work in the UK by 01/05/2005 are required to register with the Home Office under the worker registration scheme. All other EEA accession nationals who are working must register under the worker registration scheme within 30 days of starting work. Workers who are so registered will qualify for housing and welfare benefits assistance in the same way as other EEA nationals so long as they continue in work (and for up to 30 days after finishing work). Workers who finish work and who do not find work within 30 days will be required to re-register if they start back at work on some later date.

APPENDIX 4

THE CONTEXT: NATIONAL POLICY AND HOW IT IS DEVELOPING

This appendix does not aim to provide a full briefing on policy developments, but simply to summarise current and possible future developments that are of particular relevance to housing providers. Chapter 8 and appendices 6 and 7 contain sources of more detailed information and ways of keeping up-to-date.

■ General developments in immigration policy

Overall government policy can be summarised as:

- deterring and restricting the arrival of asylum claimants, especially those with unfounded claims, and bringing rates of application and removal into equilibrium
- accelerating asylum procedures and applying more severe tests in accepting applications
- containing public expenditure on asylum
- continuing and consolidating the dispersal strategy
- considering alternative 'managed migration' programmes
- promoting refugee integration and community cohesion, against the background of a 'tougher' asylum policy
- promoting 'citizenship' but at the same time restricting access to it (see below).

Some of these developments parallel those in other EU countries, where the aim is to harmonise immigration and asylum policies by 2010.

■ Asylum accommodation

Dispersal continues to be the main approach to accommodating asylum seekers. Earlier NASS contracts are being replaced from 2005 onwards. The new contracts will reflect lower expected numbers of new cases, but with a greater proportion of families. However, by 2006 the government plans to bring older cases (including those in the 'interim scheme') into the NASS programme, so the total number of service users will be about 50,000.

New contracts aim to be better value-for-money because they pass risks to providers (eg costs of void properties). There will be interim contracts which extend the current ones to 2006, then new longer-term 'Target' contracts. These will be regionally-based, so local authorities will have more chance to influence the strategy and practice of providers in their region (locations, numbers, and so on).

Government has now abandoned the controversial idea of developing accommodation centres in rural areas. It seems that this is partly because dispersal is now judged to be a success, partly because it intends to devote more resources to detention of people whose cases are rejected or 'fast-tracked', and partly because of lower numbers of applicants.

■ Acceptance of refugees through direct routes

As asylum applications decline, developed countries will be open to the accusation that the burden of dealing with refugees from countries in conflict is falling even more heavily on neighbouring, poorer countries. One way of dealing with this is to increase the use made of direct routes to refugee resettlement, such as the Gateway programme (see chapter 3). So far only limited numbers have arrived by these routes, partly because of the difficulty in persuading local authorities to take part. However, there is greater political acceptance (evident in the 2005 general election campaign) of these routes because they are seen as helping refugees who are often families with children who could not otherwise come to the UK. There may therefore be greater promotion of these alternatives.

■ Refugee status

The Home Office five-year strategy (2005) *Controlling our borders: Making migration work for Britain* proposes a change in the treatment of refugees. From now on (September, 2005) the general rule will be to give refugees temporary leave to remain for five years. After this time if circumstances in their home country have not improved they will be allowed to stay permanently. This proposal has been criticised by refugee organisations for prolonging the uncertainty which refugees face, potentially making it more difficult for them to build new lives here and integrate successfully. Some other European countries already have similar practices, however.

■ Destitution

Destitution is a problem which is reported to have grown rapidly over the last two years, for reasons set out in chapter 3. It seems likely that it will continue to grow, making integration and community cohesion policies more difficult to implement. Many refugee organisations believe that 'fast track' decision-making, and lack of effective access to proper advice and representation, are leading to poor decisions. They argue that well-founded cases are being rejected and that more people will seek to stay by whatever means because of genuine fear of returning to their home country.

One response mooted in the election campaign was to allow some groups of asylum seekers (eg whose claims have been rejected but cannot safely return home) to work. Another has been requiring people to do unpaid community work in return for 'hard case support' (see chapter 3) but this has so far only been piloted in one area. Yet another proposal is increased use of detention and a more effective removal process. However, despite many high profile cases, it is clear that removal is still ineffective and in any event is not appropriate to all cases of destitution.

The current Immigration and Asylum Bill includes a power to allow local authorities to provide 'hard case' support under s4 of the 1999 Act. If this goes ahead, and depending on how it is implemented, it may give LAs greater flexibility to help in cases of destitution.

■ Refugee integration

The 2005 policy statement *Integration Matters* received a mixed response from refugee organisations, because it recognised some important aspects of refugee integration but underplayed others. Some of the main policy changes it sets out are:

- Emphasising that if possible refugees will be integrated in the areas to which they were dispersed as asylum seekers – for example through the 'local connection' rule in relation to dispersed asylum seekers and homelessness legislation (in England and Wales).
- Recognising support needs at the point of decision, through the planned Sunrise programme (see chapter 8), during which caseworkers will develop and start to implement a Personal Integration Plan with each refugee.
- Introducing Refugee Integration Loans to cover various costs in the transition period.
- Establishing indicators to assess progress with the strategy (described in chapter 9).

Refugee organisations welcomed many aspects of the strategy, such as its recognition of the wide range of needs, funding problems, and the role of RCOs. Criticisms included its lack of recognition of the central importance of secure housing in successful integration, and the limited nature of the measures to encourage integration. Organisations such as hact have welcomed Sunrise as a useful start, but point out that the strategy does not acknowledge the need which many refugees have for longer-term support.

APPENDIX 5

PRACTICAL EXAMPLES USED IN THE GUIDE

The purpose of the practical examples is to 'bring the guide to life' by showing what can actually be achieved, inspire people to initiate services in their own areas/organisations, and provide contacts to enable them to get advice from the experience of others.

■ Collecting examples

Practical examples were collected in the following ways:

- a literature trawl – concentrating on recent examples
- an email invitation to CIH members with a registered interest in asylum/refugee issues
- a press release to the housing press (also picked up by some of the asylum information networks)
- a letter in Housing Today magazine
- responses from organisations such as hact and People for Action which hold databases on practical examples or are funding innovative approaches
- invitations to housing bodies to supply practical examples of approaches to diversity/equality and community cohesion issues for the CIH Harrogate conference.

This trawl produced well over 100 examples. Most are 'up and running', some are at the stage of funding being sought (eg bids for the hact Accommodate programme), some have only limited-period funding which was due to expire.

■ Selection of examples

The selection of examples for inclusion in the guide was based on the following criteria:

Essential

- extent to which examples illustrate the scope of the services envisaged in the guide
- whether they can be verified in one of the ways described below (see 'verifying examples')

Preferable

- examples which are already operational, with evidence of extent of use/effectiveness where available
- involvement of user groups and local communities in developing/providing services
- other innovation (eg in the way they are funded)
- whether they have been initiated by or involve housing practitioners

Relative

- geographical spread (eg from different regions of England, and from Scotland, Wales, Northern Ireland as far as possible)
- whether they have been developed by small or medium-sized organisations, and/or are outside the largest urban areas.

Reasons for *excluding* examples were:

- similar example already cited
- repetition of examples from the same organisation/locality
- project concerned is not yet 'up and running' (such projects are used as examples only where necessary to illustrate points, and no similar 'live' examples exist, and the fact is made clear in the text).

■ Describing examples

Most cannot be described in detail but have only a brief description with a non-personal source (eg a website) where further information can be found.

The kind of information which has been sought on the examples is as follows (although for reasons of space only the most pertinent of these points are included in the text):

- how did they get started?
- how are they funded?
- how do they involve service users?
- what kind of partnership arrangements are there and how were they established?
- what barriers did they overcome?
- how was the need they serve originally identified?
- how do they contribute to sustainability of communities and integration of newcomers in those communities?
- what evidence is there of usage and of successful outcomes?

Where any particular information is not provided, readers are referred to the source cited in each case.

■ Verifying examples

Except for those few examples not yet 'live' (marked in the text as 'in development') or where the example is a one-off publication or piece of research, those included have been verified in one or more ways:

- personal discussion or visit by CIH researcher, including discussions with one or more service users or with representatives of local RCOs
- existence of user surveys or an independent evaluation (eg by an academic institution, or by a funding body such as hact, JRF, or through the National Housing Awards or similar validation system)
- validation (by letter, phone call, etc) from a local RCO representing users of the service/project in question.

The questions posed in assessing an example were:

- does it appear to reach a significant number of the potential customers at which it is aimed?
- does at least one local RCO or survey of service users show that the service/project is useful/desired?
- is there concrete evidence of outcomes (eg people accommodated, personal achievement (such as people finding employment or securing benefits), user satisfaction surveys, etc)?

Figure A5.1 overleaf shows all the examples included in the three 'practical example' chapters (4, 5 and 6), some of the inclusion criteria and whether and how they were validated.

Before publication, the examples were checked as far as possible to ensure that they were still operational, descriptions were correct and that sources of further information were up to date. However, the authors cannot take any responsibility for errors such as contact details, etc which change frequently.

Figure A5.1: Practical examples

Example	Location					Type of organisation					Form of verification			
	England – metropolitan area	England – non-met area	Scotland	Wales	Northern Ireland	Local authority	Large HA (1)	Medium-sized or small HA (1)	Voluntary sector body	Other	Visit	Other systematic evaluation	Contact with users	Not applicable (see notes)
Chapter 4														
A local authority NASS contract (page 37)			✔			✔						✔		
HA provides accommodation for asylum seekers (page 37)		✔							✔			✔	✔	
Housing for refugees leaflet (page 38)		✔				✔						✔		
Advice at the point of decision (1) (page 39)		✔							✔			✔		
Advice at the point of decision (2) (page 39)		✔				✔						✔		
Encouraging refugees to stay in the area (page 40)	✔									✔				2
Refugee resettlement service (page 40)			✔			✔						✔		
Prevention of homelessness pilot (page 41)		✔				✔					✔	✔		
Hosting scheme (page 42)	✔								✔			✔		
Specialist refugee housing project (page 42)	✔							✔				✔		
Foyer to assist young asylum seekers (page 43)			✔						✔			✔		
Self-build renovation scheme (1) (page 43)	✔									✔		✔		
Self-build renovation scheme (2) (page 43)	✔									✔		✔	✔	
Effective use of private sector accommodation (1) (page 44)		✔				✔						✔		
Effective use of private sector accommodation (2) (page 44)	✔								✔	✔				3

Example	Location					Type of organisation					Form of verification			
	England – metropolitan area	England – non-met area	Scotland	Wales	Northern Ireland	Local authority	Large HA (1)	Medium-sized or small HA (1)	Voluntary sector body	Other	Visit	Other systematic evaluation	Contact with users	Not applicable (see notes)
Chapter 5														
Leicester RHA Floating Support (page 63)		✔				✔		✔			✔			
Liverpool CDS Floating Support (pages 63 & 64)	✔							✔			✔			
Gateshead Move on Service (page 63)	✔					✔					✔			
Bradford CHT Asylum Team (page 63)	✔					✔							✔	
Bournemouth Churches HA – Refugee Support team (page 63)		✔						✔			✔			
Support Service for Older Women (page 64)	✔								✔		✔			
Support service for Somali tenants (page 65)		✔					✔				✔			
Interpreter/translation service (page 65)	✔							✔			✔			
A dedicated health team (1) (page 66)	✔									✔	✔			
A dedicated health team (2) (page 66)	✔									✔			✔	
A refugee mental health project (page 67)	✔								✔		✔			
Language training through local networks (page 67)			✔						✔		✔			
ESOL awareness training (page 67)		✔				✔					✔			
Survey of needs leads to specialist service (1) (page 68)		✔								✔	✔			
Survey of needs leads to specialist service (2) (page 68)	✔									✔				2
Job-related advice in refugee centre (page 69)	✔								✔		✔			
A skill-sharing scheme (page 69)			✔					✔					✔	
Work shadowing for refugees (page 70)	✔								✔		✔			

Example	Location					Type of organisation					Form of verification			
	England – metropolitan area	England – non-met area	Scotland	Wales	Northern Ireland	Local authority	Large HA (1)	Medium-sized or small HA (1)	Voluntary sector body	Other	Visit	Other systematic evaluation	Contact with users	Not applicable (see notes)
Chapter 6														
A residents' association welcomes new migrants (page 81)		✔				✔			✔				✔	
Better informing local residents (page 82)	✔								✔		✔			
Local residents provide practical help (page 82)	✔							✔	✔				✔	
Local myth-busting leaflet (page 82)				✔					✔					2
Local residents provide practical help (page 83)	✔								✔			✔		
Providing a social centre for young refugees (page 83)				✔					✔				✔	
Forming a local network (page 84)	✔						✔	✔						3
Sharing experiences (page 84)	✔								✔				✔	
Challenging racism among young people (page 85)		✔				✔							✔	
Dealing with the media (page 85)				✔					✔					2
Citizenship project tackles asylum issues (page 85)	✔										✔			2

Note 1: large HAs are defined as those with more than 10,000 units; medium or small HAs as those with less.
Note 2: 'one-off' projects - research exercises, publications, exhibitions, etc.
Note 3: projects in development where it is too soon to have evidence of use.

APPENDIX 6

CONTACTS AND SOURCES OF FURTHER INFORMATION

This appendix gives website details of the national organisations most frequently referred to in the text, from which further contact information can be obtained. Other, more specialist contacts and websites will be found in the main text.

Organisation	Information provided	Website or other contact details
UK Government departments and directorates		
IND	research and policy information	www.ind.homeoffice.gov.uk
NASS	policy bulletins	www.ind.homeoffice.gov.uk/ (go to the section on *applying*, then *support*)
Department of Health	Information on health entitlement and asylum health issues	www.dh.gov.uk (go to *alphabetical index* and then to *asylum seekers and refugees*)
Department of Trade and Industry	Information on migrant workers' employment rights	www.dti.gov.uk
Government agencies – England		
Housing Corporation	Various relevant publications, grants, etc	www.housingcorp.gov.uk
NRU	Information on neighbour-hood renewal, social exclusion, ethnic monitoring and partnership working	www.neighbourhood.gov.uk www.renewal.net
National organisations (many are UK-wide)		
ASSET UK	UK-wide body working to improve asylum seekers' and refugees' skills and training	www.asset-uk.org.uk
Asylum Policy	Website of news and inform-ation; daily email bulletin	www.asylumpolicy.info
Asylum Support Appeals Project	Advice in contesting refusals of NASS support	No website. Contact (agencies only, not individuals): 020 8684 5972 or advice@asaproject.org.uk →

Organisation	Information provided	Website or other contact details
bmespark	Information on BME aspects of Supporting People and related topics	www.bmespark.org.uk
Connexions	Government support service for 13-19 year olds – often has relevant local projects	www.connexions.gov.uk/partnerships
Empty Homes Agency	Works with RCOs and RCHAs in projects making use of empty properties	www.emptyhomes.com
FBHO	Works with BME HAs and others to promote a diverse social housing sector	www.fbho.org.uk
hact	Research, sponsorship, advice and publications in relation to refugees and housing	www.hact.org.uk
ICAR	Navigation guides and other background material	www.icar.org.uk
International Organisation for Migration	Information and resources on migration issues	www.iomlondon.org
IPPR	National 'think tank' which researches and publishes on asylum (among other topics)	www.ippr.org.uk
Joint Council for the Welfare of Immigrants	Immigration law, information and resources	www.jcwi.org.uk
National Rent Deposit Forum	UK-wide charity supporting rent deposit schemes	www.nrdf.org.uk
RaceActionNet	Expertise and good practice in dealing with racist harassment and attacks	www.raceactionnet.co.uk
Rainer	Provider of local services for 'under-supported' young people	www.raineronline.org
Refugee Council	Campaigning, training, advice-giving national body with useful website and email bulletin	www.refugeecouncil.org.uk

→

Organisation	Information provided	Website or other contact details
Refugee Action	Independent body working with refugees through a range of local projects/services	www.refugee-action.org.uk
RETAS	UK-wide body with resources on training and employment for refugees	www.education-action.org
Shelter	Homelessness website with information on law and practice on this issue	www.homelessnessact.org.uk
Sova	Runs local volunteer projects in the field of social inclusion, and has experience working with young refugees	www.sova.org.uk
Sure Start	Government programme working with families with young children	www.surestart.gov.uk
UNHCR	General information on refugees worldwide	www.unhcr.org.uk
Government bodies and other organisations in Scotland		
Scottish Executive	Scottish Refugee Integration Forum action plan, its 2005 update and other information	www.scotland.gov.uk (go to the *people and society* section)
Communities Scotland	Awards grants and develops policy on housing and regeneration issues	www.communitiesscotland.gov.uk
Scottish Refugee Council	Advice, training, publications on asylum and refugee issues	www.scottishrefugeecouncil.org.uk
Positive Action in Housing	Enabling, casework and volunteer organisation promoting the interests of asylum seekers and refugees	www.paih.org
COSLA Refugee and Asylum Seekers Consortium	COSLA has taken over responsibility for the Scottish consortium – website contains information on asylum support and wider issues	www.asylumscotland.org.uk

→

Organisation	Information provided	Website or other contact details
Government bodies and other organisations in Wales		
Welsh Assembly Government	Policy and guidance on refugee housing and other issues (NB the housing guidance has a comprehensive list of Welsh contacts)	www.wales.gov.uk (go to *social justice and regeneration* then to *housing*)
Welsh Refugee Council	Support to asylum seekers and refugees	www.welshrefugeecouncil.org
Government bodies and other organisations in Northern Ireland		
Department for Social Development	Funding and policy information on housing and social issues	www.dsdni.gov.uk
Northern Ireland Council for Ethnic Minorities (NICEM)	Policy information and asylum/refugee services	www.nicem.org.uk
Council for Homeless Northern Ireland (CHNI)	Bulletin *Chainmail* with information on local minority communities	contact: info@chni.org.uk
Specialist housing associations and related bodies (England only)		
Refugee HA	Providers of housing and support to asylum seekers and refugees	www.refugeehousing.org.uk
ARHAG	London-centred asylum/refugee housing and support services	www.arhagatep.co.uk
Safe Haven Yorkshire	Yorkshire-centred asylum/refugee housing and support services	www.safehaven.org.uk (site under construction)
Media		
The Guardian	'Society' website has section on asylum with reports and briefings	www.society.guardian.co.uk

APPENDIX 7

KEY REPORTS AND PUBLICATIONS

Ager, A and Strang, A (2004) *The Experience of Integration: A qualitative study of refugee integration in the local communities of Pollokshaws and Islington.* Home Office Online Report 55/04 (available on their website).

Blackaby, B (2004) *Community Cohesion and Housing – A good practice guide.* CIH.

Carey-Wood, J (1997) *Meeting Refugees' Needs in Britain: the role of refugee-specific initiatives.* Home Office (available on their website).

Centrepoint (2004) *Waiting in Line: young refugees in the labour market* (see www.centrepoint.org.uk).

CIH (2003) *Providing a Safe Haven – Housing Asylum Seekers and Refugees* (available at www.cih.org/policy).

Commission for Racial Equality (2005) *Code of Practice on Racial Equality in Housing – Consultation Draft.* CRE (available on their website).

D'Onofrio, L and Munk, K (2004) *Understanding the Stranger – Final Report.* ICAR.

Dumper, H (2002) *Is it Safe Here? – Refugee women's experiences in the UK.* Refugee Action (available at www.refugee-action.org.uk).

The Guardian (2001) *Welcome to Britain – A special investigation into asylum and immigration* (available on their website and also as a paper version).

Hact (2003) *Between NASS and a Hard Place.* Hact.

Home Office (2005) *Integration Matters: A national strategy for refugee integration* (available on their website).

ICAR (2004) *Media Image, Community Impact – Assessing the impact of media and political images of refugees and asylum seekers on community relations in London.* ICAR.

Lemos, G (2005) *The Search for Tolerance – Challenging and changing racist attitudes and behaviour among young people.* JRF.

LGA and others (2002) *Guidance on Community Cohesion* (available at www.lga.gov.uk).

LGA and others (2004) *Community Cohesion – an action guide: guidance for local authorities* (available at www.lga.gov.uk).

Lupton, M and Perry, J (2004) *The Future of BME Housing Associations*. CIH.

Marsh, A *et al* (2005) *Crossing the Housing and Care Divide: A guide for practitioners*. CIH for JRF.

Moorehead, C (2005) *Human Cargo: A Journey among Refugees*. Chatto and Windus.

Mullins, D *et al* (2004) *Empowering Communities, Improving Housing: Involving black and minority ethnic tenants and communities*. ODPM (available on their website).

National Audit Office (2005) *National Asylum Support Service: The provision of accommodation for asylum seekers* (see www.nao.gov.uk).

Roberts, K and Harris, J (2002) *Disabled people in refugee and asylum-seeking communities*. Policy Press for JRF, York.

Robinson, D *et al* (2004) *How Housing Management can Contribute to Community Cohesion*. CIH.

Scottish Refugee Integration Forum (2005) *Action Plan – Progress Report*. Scottish Executive (available from their website).

Welsh Assembly Government (2005) *Asylum Seekers and Refugees: Guidance for housing and related service providers in Wales*. WAG (available from their website).

Wren, K (2004) *Building Bridges: Local responses to the resettlement of asylum seekers in Glasgow*. Scottish Centre for Research on Social Justice, University of Glasgow.

Zetter, R (2005) *Still Surviving and Now Settling – Refugees, asylum seekers and a renewed role for housing associations*. Housing Corporation (available on their website).

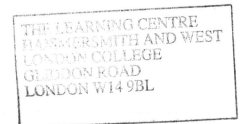

THE LEARNING CENTRE
HAMMERSMITH AND WEST
LONDON COLLEGE
GLIDDON ROAD
LONDON W14 9BL